Heaven Has No Regrets

Tessa Shaffer

Dedication

This book is dedicated to anyone who's ever lost someone they love. The truth is—you'll hate to hear this—but it does get better. You have to work through it though; grief is like the chapters in a book, each page needs to be faced before it can be turned. But eventually, a new chapter of your life will begin. Remember that the past is always gone, but the future is yours to write.

This book is also dedicated to anyone who hasn't lost someone they love. The truth is—you'll hate to hear this—but one day you will. Hold fewer grudges and give more hugs. Make the most of every moment, because this very moment is all we have. Keep your heart open to live and love with no regrets.

**Most importantly this is for her.
Everything has always been
And will forever be
For her.**

The End

Ends meet beginnings.
Always.
No matter what.

Death takes all persons but once, yet it comes several times before that—to tease, to torture, and to taunt. Death will take away pieces of you that you've never been able to keep, like your heart. And the death around you will kill you slower than any painful, real death, ever could.

You'll be left begging for the end, when your new beginning has just begun. . . .

. . . .

       I sit outside, alone, in the middle of an empty driveway, in front of a house that isn't mine, in a world that is no longer mine. Only when I look around and try to uncross my eyes from the spinning do I truly know where I am.

I'm here.
But it doesn't make any sense.
Nothing makes any sense anymore.

I look down to see clothes latching on to me, and they too are not mine.
       They're hers.
And right now, it feels like everything must have always been hers.
       Everything.

Why else would I feel as if I had nothing right now?

       Sitting on the cold earth with knees bent pointing to the sky, and hands grasping at the broken pavement below me, I feel dizzy. I'm clinging to the ground, begging dirt and gravel to wedge underneath my fingernails and to help me keep the Earth from spinning.

       I just need the Earth to stop spinning right now.

       Because my world has stopped.

       But as much as I can't take the spinning, I'd be waiting forever for it to slow down. And I can't help feeling like forever is too long. And I can't do it . . . I can't take the spinning.

There's no way I'm doing this . . .

       Not without her.

And there's that sinking feeling again. It knocks the wind right out of me like the universe just shrunk into a heavy ball and hurled itself right into my stomach, I'm coughing up snot and tears and choking for air. I hold my middle and gasp for breath in between choking cries and I wonder when it will stop feeling like this. When will I be able to take the constant punches of reality? Am I ever going to be able to breathe the same again, or will I only be holding my breath and bracing for the next blow . . .

I don't know, and I am resigned to this new know-nothing-ness.

My legs are weak, but they are all I have, and so I hug them close to my chest and create a little balled-up girl on the harsh blacktop. My arms squeeze at my legs as tight as I would ever squeeze her, and through tears I can see the tops of my kneecaps are skinned and bleeding. Even the bright red, the blood . . . reminds me of her, and I can't do this. How can I survive in a world that will only ever be "her"—without her?

I hold on to myself tight and close my eyes. Words from some distant memory play back, soothing me. *"It's okay, it's okay, it's okay . . ."*

And I quiet my screams, both inside and out, to hear these silent words better. My thoughts are wrapped so tightly around me that they hurt. And my arms are shaking trying to keep hold of my own legs. I can't trust my legs, they feel like they could start running and never stop but at the same time like they will disintegrate as soon as I put weight on them.

I focus on the words, *"It's okay,"* repeating them in my head like some worn-out mantra. And then my feet, with a sudden motherly instinct, begin to rock me, slowly lifting themselves up and down from the blacktop. They are rocking me back and forth in my tightly self-hugging ball. For a moment I am soothed. I lessen my grip on my legs and am living in a moment of "it's okay"s. Over and over again I rock to this one thought. My head is bowed down surrendering to exhaustion and rocking back and forth tucked into my knees.

And then, once I'm quiet and calm, I can hear that the voice re-playing in my head, telling me it's okay, soothing me, is hers.

But how can it be her voice . . .

And as soon as I acknowledge it, in that very second, it's gone. And so is the calm. I start to cry again, a panicked plea. My hands reaching, clawing at the broken gravel beneath me. I open my eyes, squinting through tears, reaching to see her.

She has to be here.
How she can be everywhere, in everything, but not here right now.

She's not here.
I'm alone.
Outside in an empty world.

I don't remember how I got to this house or why I am sitting in this empty driveway. I've been here before, but not like this. It's like I'm stuck in a photograph, and I'm looking at myself in a picture of a moment that I was never in. Even though I am wholeheartedly refusing this moment I can't stop from being in it. But refusing to believe something doesn't make it unreal. My eyes are shut tight to this moment and when I open them I am still here, faded as can be, and the day is just beginning.

I look down again, and I start pulling at her black mesh shorts that I'm wearing. I remember these shorts from her wearing them a hundred times before and I've never had one feeling towards them, but today . . . today, I hate them. With the hatred that my arms have claimed, I pull at the ends of the fabric trying to rip seams apart. Even if it leaves my pale thighs naked, I don't care, I can't stand seeing them right now. Not without her in them. I'm undeserving of wearing these clothes. I don't even know why I thought for a second that I was. I just wanted to be blanketed in her, and her clothes are all I have. I stretch the leg opening of the shorts as far as it will go and I give up. I'm not good enough for this cheap material and I can't help but feel like I'll never be good enough for anything ever again.

I pull at my elbows and hug my arms back into my stomach and I feel like I'm going to throw up. There's a constant movement from my stomach to my throat. Tears are coming out of my eyes and my mouth, and I can't stop choking on the spit of tears. The sunrise is coming soon and someone will eventually find me lying on the black pavement like a finished earthworm because this sunrise coming up and around, this very first sunrise, will absolutely kill me.

Now, I'm just waiting for death again.

As much as I wish the sun to stay dark and still forever, I can't stop the sunrise from coming. Just like I couldn't stop her from leaving. Sun streaks break across the sky in pinks and oranges, and clouds are sweeping in gentle brushstrokes, the kind that make you think that God is a painter and all painters must be gods, but I can't keep from thinking that it's got to be the ugliest freaking sunrise I've ever seen. So I close my eyes and shield myself from the life the sky has to offer. Just give up, I beg the sun behind my tears, just give up because life is over. She's gone. I'm alone, and I'll never be another thing without her . . .

And then it hits me again, just as hard as it did the first time and the time after that: She's really lost and I don't know how I'm to keep from ever looking for her again. All of me wants to start walking. Just start looking for her.

But all I can do is sit.

Helpless.

I have an inch of hope left in me, and I wish nothing more than for it to just die too. Hope only confuses me. Hope tells me that this can't be right. Not now. I'm not ready. Hope lets me think I can flip the coin again, call tails this time. Put money on red, not black. I changed my mind. I'm not ready. Re-do. Please re-do this life. I'm not ready. And hope makes me wait for the curtain to be pulled back and the confetti to fall, and for the hidden camera guy to reveal himself and to tell me that this was the newest reality show and I am now America's biggest chump. Make me a fool, make me a guppy, just make me anything but hopeful.

Even though there's no confetti, I can't stop waiting for it.

Mid-summer air sticks to my lungs and burns like the coldest winter. My chest feels tighter with every short empty breath. Pain

12

fills the center of me and spreads up through my throat and I wonder if my insides are imploding. My heart is seizing in a way that makes me think this has all been one long heart attack.

Maybe I'm not really here.

Maybe I am gone too.

I only know that I'm still alive because it would be too perfect for me not to be. And I squeeze my eyes shut hard. My eyes hemorrhage tears as thick as blood, and I swear I can feel God staring right at me. Right through to my empty heart.

And I hope He just forgets about me soon.

I hope He's fucking happy now.

But there's that devil of a word again—hope . . .

Faith

As soon as she realized she was breathing, Faith frantically awoke from her dreams as if she had fallen asleep by accident.

Or been alive by accident.

She gasped for another breath and then a smaller gulp of air while her hands were palm down against the cold stale white sheets. Unpainted fingertips bent into the wrinkles of the white cloth fabric below her waist and she opened her eyes wide enough to scare a child, if there were a child there. But there wasn't. No one was there. Just her. And although only fifteen, Faith was no child. She was already a young adult. With all of the worst responsibilities, pains, and disappointments of a grown-up, but with the capability of a child to change nothing about any of them.

She held her breath and felt a complete wave of both disappointment and anxiety, as if she were about to drown and those were the last times her lungs would fill with warm comfort. Her eyes quickly scanned the empty room for clues of where she was and her arms pushed themselves against the plastic covered mattress beneath her as she tried for just a moment to sit up.

Her eyes focused on a piece of paper hanging on the clipboard directly in front of her and she knew this was no dream. This was real. And she wished herself back to sleep. Once she realized where she was, it was confirmed that every breath for the rest of the day would bring her overwhelming pain, and it was exactly like drowning.

Her life was a lot like drowning.

She sighed and her arms gave out in pain, her head giving a solid punch to the pillow beneath her that was curved to the shape of her matted dirty blond hair. Her back, her kidneys, her stomach, and her heart all had a broken aching to them.

A dull constant, empty ache.

She was eternally internally broken.

Her pale body was ninety-six pounds, half wrapped in a cotton gown that had been washed so many times that she felt like she was naked. Faith thought for just a moment about the other people that may have worn that exact hospital gown as she straightened out the wrinkles down her front. Her fingers found a stain on the fabric near her left side in the shape of nothing, and she wondered if the beige blob on the hip of the fabric used to, at one point in time, be somebody's bright red blood.

Probably.

Her eyelids gave a shrug as she sighed, and she tried not to imagine the number of small bodies that may have died in this exact piece of white cotton gown with faded blue diamonds.

And now, thanks to that blob . . .

For the rest of the day,
  She would try not to think about dying.

Makenzie

Her thumb and index finger were masked with chipped pink nail polish as they squeezed a patch of her belly fat beneath her shirt. Makenzie made a puckered frown at herself as she let the skin go and squinted in an effort to remember where in her room she hid her last pack of menthol cigarettes. While she thought about it, she bit down on the very edge of one of her nails.

Behind the dresser.

No.

Insider her pillow case.

No.

Side pocket of her book bag.

Bingo.

She yanked a lighter off her dresser top, sitting beside a candle with a burnt wick that she wasn't ever allowed to light. She looked at the shut door to her room and thought about how her dad and stepmom would yell at her for lighting candles, as if she were attempting arson by filling the house with a lovely floral scent, and she lit the candle defiantly.

She walked over to the window beside her bed to ignite her menthol cancer stick. She quietly opened the window just enough to let the outside world in, and closed her mouth around the tan end of the cigarette holding on to it loosely with her left hand. Her right hand held up the lighter in front of her cigarette and she flicked the red Bic lighter once *chhk*, and then twice *chhk*, only sparking it. She sighed and hammered her right thumb down harder against the flint wheel on to the little red pad with success. Her eyes widened at the fire and when the sparks flew and the flame grew taller she brought the lighter closer to the dry stick of tobacco. She crossed her eyes down the sight of her nose to watch the end of the cigarette glow and it lit joy inside of her. She sucked the end of the cigarette like a straw, slowly inviting the flame in further. The little bones in the base of her neck cracked, relaxed, as she took a deep breath of toxic air. She'd been breathing all day, but that was the first time she had really noticed. She slid the lighter in the front pocket of her jeans as she leaned over and exhaled out the window.

She thought about everyone's life but her own as she sat staring out of the second story window. Cars passed below on the street in front of her house and she caught glimpses of the drivers' profiles.

There was a 40-something lady driver with short hair in a red mini-van and Makenzie pretended that the lady's passenger seat wasn't empty. That maybe instead Makenzie were sitting right there next to her with her feet on the dash and asking that lady if she liked the nail polish on the right foot or the left foot better. She imagined the lady would laugh at her un-matching but well-painted toes and they would go somewhere and do girly things like pick out a dress for her school's upcoming fall homecoming dance.

Makenzie realized staring out her window and seeing cars with would-be moms drive by, how much she missed having her own mom around to do those things with.

She took another drag of her cigarette thinking about how in that exact moment in the world, her mom was another state over somewhere else right now driving a mom car and being a mom to other little girls.

Little girls who would grow up with both a mom and a dad.

Little girls who would never have to know how lucky they were.

Makenzie thought about her parents, how they both had remarried and become different people than what they were before. Makenzie couldn't stop feeling like she were just the product of a past that neither of her parents wanted to remember. But she couldn't stop reminding her mom and dad of their past. Just by breathing, she provoked a painful connection to each other and a reminder of the people that they both used to be.

The people that they both hated.

She didn't mean to.

But she couldn't stop.

She knew that they hated each other. Because they did absolutely nothing to hide it. She could even see their hate for each other in the way that they looked at her sometimes. Every now and then, she could see the look in their eyes when they tried hard to bite their tongues from saying things like *"you're acting just like your mother."* Or *"Where'd you learn that from, your father?"* She knew that she possessed certain traits of each of her parents, and she liked to think that at one time they might have been in love and cooed over the fact that their little girl had her father's hair and her mother's smile. But now that she had her dad's sarcastic attitude and her mom's headstrong defiance, it was different. Now she was just constantly reminding them of why it all ended. And because of this, she knew that as long as she let all of her natural traits, quirks, and full personality show, that she would never be perfect in the eyes of either of her parents.

She would never be all that they hoped for.

She knew that she wasn't enough. She wasn't enough to keep them together then. And she wasn't enough to keep their attention now.

Because, both of her parents already had newer children.

Better children.

Children who wouldn't be royally fucked up and ripped in half by a divorce. Children who wouldn't live with and receive life training from the "enemy."

Makenzie took another drag of menthol, and the smoke she inhaled burned her throat. Her lungs, however, felt fine. They felt like if they could, they would have been smiling.

The next car that drove by was going at least twice the speed limit. She couldn't see how many people were in the car, but she wished more than anything for there to be a seat left for her. She didn't care if they were turning left or right at the stop sign at the end of her road, she wouldn't care if they were going straight into the sun, she just wanted to be going somewhere too. She wished to be anywhere but on the windowsill where she sat. If the window were open any further the house might just have spit her out. That house hated her and she could feel it. Or maybe it was just accumulated hate that the house held that she could feel around her, but she couldn't take it.

She didn't belong there.

She was so over feeling like a burden to her dad and stepmom. Like her entire existence was such an inconvenience to them. She hated that she needed to be sorry for taking up so much air. More than anything, she hated that they wanted her to be someone that she wasn't. *"Grow up, already,"* they'd say, always complaining that she wasn't mature enough.

But growing up isn't just an attitude, it's a lifelong process. It's a process that they forget took them some thirty years to achieve. And even then, Makenzie's mom would still say that her dad wasn't mature enough now.

Still.

So what the hell did they want from her, she was only fifteen.

The truth was, she didn't want to grow up, because every adult she ever met would tell her "*enjoy high school, 'cause these are the best years of your life.*" But she didn't want to grow up if it meant the best times of her life would be over, how was she supposed to deal with her own mortality like that when she was just starting to become who she was.

And even though she didn't want to grow up, from the pure teenage principle of feeling like she might die if she did, she honestly did try to. Because she wanted to make her parents proud more than she wanted to live, so if it meant killing off her childhood, she would eventually appease them. But it was almost like her dad and stepmom, as much as they'd complain about her not being grown up, they wouldn't let her. They may as well have been holding her down and slapping her with her own hands saying *"stop hitting yourself."* Anytime she tried doing grown-up things, they'd freak out on her.

She wasn't responsible yet because they wouldn't give her enough chances to practice being responsible. They didn't give her enough opportunity to fail, and to learn from failure. She wasn't allowed to have a cell phone, she couldn't have a Facebook, and she'd never have a car. How was she ever going to learn the whole responsibility thing if she was always shut down from the opportunity to be in charge of any small aspect of her life?

She took another drag of her cigarette and thought about how much she hated how her dad acted like growing up was just a phase that Makenzie would get over. He didn't understand that she was trying to both discover and create herself and that she hoped that she wasn't just a phase. She hoped that being herself wouldn't just pass her by. Maybe parts of growing up were a phase, maybe she'd go through a few phases before getting to the be-all and end-all boring desk job that would finally allow society to approve of her. But she just wanted to think that whoever she was, in whatever phase she was in, on whatever level of maturity or immaturity that she was loved.

She just wanted to be loved.

In all of her immature imperfections.

She felt something in her stomach that reminded her of humiliation, and the cigarette in her left hand was burning down quicker with every puff and her fingertips could feel the heat of it ending. Her room was starting to collect some of the spirals of thin smoky ribbons. Makenzie watched as a slight breeze made them glide further into her room, weaving and dancing around each other. She ashed the end of the cigarette out the window and squished the filter between her fingers until it threw up its cherry. She rolled her eyes at nothing and then ripped the cigarette filter into the tiniest pieces it would let her before she buried them in a half-used tissue in the bottom of the trash can beside her bed.

She went back to her dresser top and picked up a bottle of light pink Cherry Blossom room spray and squirted three mists into the direct center of her world. She waved her arms through the mists of fragrance like she was trying to slap fight the spritz of sweet scent into marrying with the smoke in the room. She looked at the candle that she had lit on her dresser, knowing that if her dad complained about it smelling like smoke that she could blame it on the candle and get into less trouble for trying to set the house on fire than she would have for smoking cigarettes. She leaned over the pink candle and felt the warmth of the flame on her nose.

She closed her eyes.

She made a wish.

And with one breath she blew the flame out.

Faith

There was an 8.5" x 11" pain scale questionnaire in her hospital room hanging from a white pushpin on the bulletin board beyond her feet. The pin was weak enough that it let the laminated piece of paper hang loose and sway back and forth when anyone walked by. She had already been forced to look at these pain scales enough to memorize the text and graphics on them, and now there was one waving at her every day.

The bold cartoony title read *How Do You Feel Today? Wong-Baker FACES Pain Rating Scale* with smiley faces under it that were numbered 1–10.

One was happy.

Ten was not.

And all of the Faces in between just looked silly. The nurses and doctors that would come in that day would all ask her how she was feeling from one to ten. If she ever said words or feelings other than a number they would point to the chart, explain the faces, and ask her again. They had to compare all of her numbers every day to the numbers from the day before including her blood pressure, her blood counts, and those stupid smiley face numbers.

Faith's exact face could have been on that chart and she still wouldn't have picked it. Because she didn't want to admit how she really felt.

She couldn't.

Not words or cartoon faces could explain the pain she guarded inside.

Even the saddest face frowning in pain with tears coming out of its eyes on the scale at 10 looked like it had at least a morphine of hope on the horizon. And more than that, all of the stupid yellow faces on the chart all looked like men. Bald, snarky, yellow men with big cheeks.

None of the faces looked like women.

Or girls.

And none of the faces looked like a scale reference of the pain that a little girl felt after her dad walked out on her family. None of the yellow faces even came close to the pain that two months of Faith waiting for him to come home felt like.

The pain of realizing she wasn't worth coming back for.

On a pain scale from one to ten, that would have been the pain of one hundred stupid smileys.

Faith felt a wave of anxiety cross her stomach. Her insides spasm-ed at the thought of being discarded. But that's exactly what she was. She was left by one of only two people out of the billions of people on Earth who created her. Who were if nothing more, supposed to at the least hold on to her for a little while.

But he folded.

He abandoned her.

Without warning.

Without reason.

Faith thought about how it would have hurt her less if he had just died in front of her. What an awful thought for a child to have to agree to. To have to even think about. She nodded to herself, in her hospital bed thinking about it now, and thought about how at least then, if she would have watched him fade away, she could have at least seen what happened. She wouldn't have to constantly try to picture him sneaking out of a dark house and never looking back. At least if he were dead, the pain would have had a label. Death would be his excuse for leaving her. And no one would have questioned that reason for leaving, because people die and leave things they don't want to all the time.

But he left her on purpose.

It was his choice, not God's.

She wished when he disappeared that it could have just been to Heaven. And at least if that had happened, she would have scars that made sense and she wouldn't have to try so hard with every breath not to hate him. At least then she would know where he was and that he for sure wasn't coming back, but she could at least assume that if he were in Heaven that he still loved her.

But instead, it was the opposite.

She had only fifteen years and nothing to show for it. Fifteen years of her dad telling her that he loved her, all erased by his leaving.

Without a goodbye.

Without a note.

Without a goddamn thing.

The only words she had to hold on to now were the ones that echoed in the silence of an unsaid goodbye.

"She wasn't good enough."

She wasn't worth a goodbye. She wasn't even worthy of the time, the feelings, or the smallest energy of an explanation.

She wasn't enough.

She would never be enough.

And she wondered what she could have done better. What about her made it so easy for him to leave? What made her so un-lovable? And she worried more than anything, if everyone else could already see it. Was she the only one who didn't know? But, it seemed like at least parts of her knew how meaningless her life was, because most of her body was giving up on her now too.

Lying flat in the hospital bed, Faith thought about the fact that her dad could live without her. That he chose it. He preferred it best. And she wondered, maybe, if he had known how sick she was, if he would have come back.

But she knew it wouldn't have changed anything.

Because if he cared about her at all, he would have never left.

She reminded herself, holding on to the sickness of pain in her right side, that leaving someone isn't a symptom of love.

Leaving is the exact opposite of love.

Makenzie

She flipped the covers off in one swoop folding them over themselves like a perfect omelet on her bed, and she thought about what she'd wear to school that day. She settled on her favorite jeans, the only pair that fit her right, that made her feel like she belonged in them. She thought about wearing a new T-shirt that she had traded one of her girlfriends for but her dad would freak if he saw her wearing something that wasn't hers. He acted as though trading clothing with friends was the same as stealing, as if she had gone into a department store and traded rags to riches while in the dressing room. He didn't understand teenage girls at all. And even though her stepmom had at one time probably been a teenage girl, she would for sure have accused Makenzie of stealing that shirt from the mall too. And she didn't want lessons or lectures today, she just wanted to be loved.

She got dressed and stood in front of the dresser mirror staring herself down. She pulled at the gaps that her jeans had in between her thighs and in the pocket where her butt should be and made a face at herself in the mirror as if her reflection could do anything about the awkwardness that losing ten pounds did to her wardrobe.

She was a teenager, everything felt awkward.

She turned around again to face front and pushed her A-cup bra together and shrugged. She looked at the time and knew she'd be waiting all day for her ass to fill out her jeans and her boobs to fill out her tank top, so she pulled the hoodie over her head. Both hands rose to her head, fingers spread like the teeth of combs and quickly calmed down her frizzing strawberry blonde hair. She zoomed in closer to her reflection to evaluate the progress that her overnight face cream had made. She squinted her eyes scanning for imperfections and without losing eye contact with herself she reached a hand for the eyeliner and quickly traced above her lashes. She traded the eyeliner in her makeup bag for the black mascara and while she coated her lashes she also willed them to grow longer. Makenzie grabbed her favorite makeup essential, the eyelash curler, and slid her fingers through the scissor-like openings. She held it with the power some might feel holding a handgun and carefully lined up her just wet lashes in the crosshairs of the curler and slowly pushed the ends together to crimp her lashes upward while her eye widened and was witness to the whole thing.

She brushed her hair for the third and final time and then grabbed her body spray off the dresser, spraying quick mists in front of her before walking through them, like a model.

On the way downstairs she passed her dad and reminded him about lunch money. He acted as if she had just applied for a loan and he needed to check her credit history.

She made a face.

He made a face.

And then he sighed as if he already knew that she'd been skipping lunch every day that week and saving her lunch money that he had been giving her for a new pair of jeans, and he gave her three dollars anyways.

Faith

She lay on her back, defenseless against the world. She wished more than anything that she could have just curled up on her side into the fetal position, but the IVs and cords running into her wouldn't let her bend like that, they all made it hard to feel safe. The beeping of the Hospital had become a separate heartbeat than her own, but both continuously let her know that she was still alive.

Still.

She looked out her large bedside window and wished that the curtains were shut. She saw a blue sky that lightened the bright yellow walls of her hospital room and she tried to think about what she might be doing if she weren't lying there still right then. Hershey Pennsylvania was self-proclaimed as the "Sweetest Place on Earth," but less advertised than chocolate, it was also home to one of the state's largest Children's Hospitals. The streets lined with Hershey Kiss-shaped streetlamps that led excited children and families on vacation to chocolate tour rides and rollercoasters were the same exact streets that led anxious children and families to X-rays and MRIs on the worsts days of their lives.

Chocolate was being created on the same street that childhood diseases were being diagnosed. And that was life. The sweetest of sensations and the deepest of devastations often live next door to each other.

Faith could only feel the devastation in the air, but her mom would come in to sit with her every day and ask how she felt with the kind of excitement someone might have for an expectant mother, *"How are you feeling?"* As if Faith's cheeks were glowing.

But they weren't.

She was tired.

She was trapped in a little room.

In a little bed.

In a little gown.

And everything around her smelled like the kind of disinfected clean that made her wonder how clean it really was. It made her wonder how foul had it been before that they needed to clean it with a concoction of chemicals that smelled so unearthly strong.

It smelled like cancerous potpourri.

Faith was so weak that if she reached up to the table tray next to her for a glass of water, she would be trying to catch her breath for half an hour. She was not allowed to get out of bed, but for most of the day she couldn't move anyways.

When she did move, it was only to use the bathroom.

And when she would go to the bathroom, there would be blood.
Again.

And there would be a lot of it.

And she would have to call a nurse to tell them. They were making her save every evacuation of her bowels in a bedpan over the toilet. They needed to see them, to look at how disgusting she really was. They made her show them, that despite the hours of painful tests and trials of different medications, her insides were still bleeding.

Still.

How she felt, was that she was dying.

From the inside out.

And doing it in the most uncomfortable and embarrassing way possible.

Makenzie

She dialed the only seven numbers in a row that would promise her the response that she needed, and her Grandma answered the phone smiling, "Yellowwwww?"

Her grandparents didn't have an answering machine, and they didn't need one because someone was always there. And to Makenzie, nothing could replace that feeling.

"Oh Hi, Kenzie, how are you doing?" it was the feeling of someone getting excited over her, over nothing. Everyone deserved that feeling.

Makenzie was glad that her Grandmother had answered the phone because she didn't like to unload on her Grandfather. Her Grandma asked how she was doing in a way that wrapped her voice around Makenzie and suddenly she was already doing better, so she just said that she was okay and returned the question. Makenzie had called to complain about life but she didn't need to complain anymore, she just needed to feel heard. Her Grandma said that she was the, "Same old, same old" with a sarcastic emphasis on the "old" and she asked Makenzie, "Have you heard from your cousin yet?" As if Faith were missing.

Makenzie had asked "Yet? Why?" as if there was some imaginary deadline not met. What her Grandma said next awoke Makenzie's insides.

"Faith is in the Hospital. . ." Her Grandma's voice trailed off like saying those words exhausted her.

Ten million thoughts ran through Makenzie's head and they all had the same word repeatedly representing each of them, *"Fuck. Fuck. Fuck. Fuck."* Her hands were shaking like the inside little bones of her fingers needed to evacuate her body. Like they knew something that the rest of her didn't.

She didn't want to hear her Grandma repeat those words again, but she couldn't keep a *"What . . ."* from falling out of her mouth.

"Faith is at the Hospital but don't worry because I'm sure the doctors will help her and . . . at least she is getting the rest she needs." And Makenzie wished she was sitting in Grandma's kitchen right then instead of 25 miles away. Because if she were, her Grandma would have cradled her head like a baby's and pulled her in for a hug. One of those Grandma hugs that ended in a long squeeze and a kiss on the head.

And then Makenzie did what most people can't help but do when someone they love is in the hospital, she thought about the last time she saw Faith and her mind added a painful *"what if that was it."*

What if that was the last time.

The last time Makenzie saw her, Faith looked like shit.

She knew it, everyone knew it.

Makenzie remembered Faith trying to stand up from Grandma's couch and wobbling as she grabbed her side. Makenzie remembered how she helped Faith back to the couch and made her lie down. Faith was eight months older than her, but Makenzie never felt so protective than she did after Faith started to get sick. Makenzie remembered brushing the hair off Faith's forehead over and over again, asking her in the most caring, empathetically blunt way, *"What's wrong with you?"*

Makenzie hated thinking about it now, but she should have known then. She should have taken her to the Hospital herself when Faith looked up at her that day with hopeless eyes and said that she didn't know.

Makenzie should have known then that it was bad.

Because Faith always knew everything.

Makenzie put the phone down and felt something in her stomach that reminded her of regret.

Faith

A white lab coat came into the room and Faith prepared as best she could for whatever he could possible say next. He was a new Doctor she had never seen before. She didn't know what that would mean.

Faith's mom sat next to her in a square hospital chair and put a book down once she saw the man approach. He looked anxious, but maybe he just had a long morning of coffee.

Faith hoped that because he was a new doctor that he wouldn't start by asking *"when all this started"*, like she wasn't interviewed by two handfuls of doctors and nurses already and as if it weren't written on her chart. She hated when the doctors asked *"when it all started,"* because Faith's mom would measure the time from when Faith got sick and remember it in direct reference to the time when her dad left. She hated that the two events were related in any way.

Faith's mom scooted to the end of the square seat as the Doctor said, "We need to discuss a very serious subject," and he continued, "We need an answer to this question rather . . . quickly." With only a few days in the Hospital, Faith already knew that nothing happened quickly. What was the sudden emergency in his voice?

Her mom asked with hope, "Does this mean you know what's wrong?"

The question of "what was wrong with her" was already echoing in Faith's head from her own emotions. A question that she asked herself so often, that just thinking the words had carved deep grooves out of her self-worth.

The Doctor reacted, "Not quite, but we should be finding out final details soon."

Faith's mom asked, "When exactly is soon?"

"We will know for sure after a few more tests . . ." the Doctor took a deep breath to continue and Faith sighed at the thought of more tests.

More.
Still.

She hoped that he just meant more blood tests. She couldn't take any more scoping or scanning. And she certainly would not ever agree to another barium swallow X-ray again in her life, now that she knew what that was.

How it tasted.

The drink that was thicker than milk but thinner than a milkshake. The drink that the nurses asked her to pick a flavor of as if to make it seem like it was her choice, something she wanted. The pink illusion of strawberry. The room temperature cream liquid that from the moment it sat in her mouth curdled her tongue. Her tongue unwilling to push itself against the barium sulfate milkshake, hesitant to have it meet any of her taste buds, before insisting it slowly down her throat. It took the effort of her whole face to swallow one gulp. And one swallow, once downed, produced the kind of nausea from the bottom of her belly that sounded an alarm to her whole body, recognizing the makeup of the solution that she just ingested as absolute poison.

One swallow would have been too much.

But she had to drink a Big Gulp Styrofoam container of it. The exact same size that New York City had banned, she now had to drink, loaded with far worse things than sugar. And she had to drink it continually for 90 minutes. NINETY minutes. And hour and a half of swallowing and gagging and trying not to vomit while she poisoned her own body with a solution to make her insides glow in order for the doctors to see what was wrong with her. Her insides opened up and bled more at just the thought of it.

And the nurses would check on her, to keep her drinking. Faith knew that they were only extra nice and gentle with her because they knew they had just given her poison. The test was so bad that even the nurses' faces scrunched up when they came to check on her. They knew. And they tried to help her, whisper her advice: *Don't smell the liquid. Don't look at the liquid. Don't even think about the liquid. Just drink it. Chug some every fifteen minutes. And then breathe. Don't think about the next fifteen minutes. Just breathe. And whatever she did. . . . Don't vomit. Do not gag to the point of vomit. Because if she vomited, they warned her nicely, the test results would be un-usable. If she vomited, she would have to start all over.*

She couldn't take any more tests like that.

Enough already.

But the tests, just like Faith, were never enough. The Doctor continued quickly, "But right now, I need permission from you to give your daughter a blood transfusion."

"Does she really need a blood transfusion?" Faith's mom's face looked disgusted as if Faith would have to drink the blood rather than have it pumped into her veins through a tube.

The Doctor walked closer to Faith and he put his arm on the heart rate monitor that Faith had been hooked up to for days and explained, "We ran some of her latest blood through the lab for a Troponin Test and found very high levels. When the heart is stressed or damaged it releases proteins into the blood, and the levels were consistent with mild heart attacks. Troponin levels can remain high for one, even two weeks after a heart attack . . . have you had any chest pains? Has your heart been hurting you?" The Doctor looked at Faith.

Faith nodded, truthfully.
{Her heart was hurting.}

"We need to alleviate the stress on her heart immediately so it doesn't happen again. And the best way we can do that is to supply more blood."

Faith's mom rubbed her face with her right hand, "Okay. But can I just give her my blood? What about diseases that she could get from other people's blood? I just don't want her getting sick from anything else . . . I just …"

He put his hand on Faith's IV stand and said in the most impatient way, "It would take days to draw enough blood from you and screen it before Faith would be able to benefit. She needs it now. We have her type in the Hospital and it can be upstairs in just a few minutes. . . ."

Faith shrugged and nodded her head at the Doctor, approving. If he really wanted to save her, she would let them try at least. After all, it was a teaching Hospital, they had plenty of other opportunities to let her die.

Faith's mom shook her head in sadness that Faith's heart was as weak as the Doctor said, but she said "Yes," signing the paper on the clipboard, approving the blood transfusion. As soon as Faith's mom handed the pen back to the Doctor, he was out the door.

Faith wished he could have told her more about her heart and what was going on before he disappeared. Doctors always disappear so quickly. She flipped her head to the other side of the bed looking away from her mom and instead at the doorway, watching footsteps in the hallway, waiting for her new blood. Waiting for them to try and save her. She thought about how much blood she lost, and how much more she would lose before they could tell her what was wrong with her. Getting blood might sound like a fix for the doctors based on all her counts and numbers, but Faith knew it was just a Band-Aid.

The loss of blood seemed like a trivial symptom of her life. Because she knew that it wouldn't be long until she was worried about losing the blood they gave her. It wouldn't be long until she was shitting out someone else's blood from inside her.

She knew all the blood they gave her would just turn into waste.
It would all just be a waste in the end.

Makenzie

"FAITH!" Makenzie shouted through the phone commandingly like a police officer yelling "freeze!" as if she needed to stop Faith from whatever she was doing. As if Faith weren't strapped to a hospital bed with tubes of blood, air, and medicine going into her.

"Hello?" Faith sounded far away in more ways than one and Makenzie couldn't help but be upset at her. How could she not warn Makenzie that this was happening? How could she not call her to tell her? How could she not need her?

"Why are you in there? Why didn't you tell me? You're in the Hospital and I'm the last to fucking know?" Makenzie's voice cracked and she swallowed, pausing to give Faith a chance to respond. Faith was Makenzie's only constant left. The only one that was always there, and she couldn't help but panic thinking about that changing. Thinking about anything else changing right now made her nauseated.

"I've only been here since Monday," Faith said without any emotion and it made Makenzie even more upset. She was never supposed to be in the hospital at all.

"You should have called me, man, nobody told me, or I would have been there." Just then Makenzie wanted to cry, the feeling of not being right there beside her best friend for the last two days, had helplessness rising up her throat like acid reflux.

"Well, I just came in for another stupid test, but they wouldn't let me leave this time. I didn't tell anyone, my cell phone died and this is the first time I even knew there was a phone in the room." Faith sighed, "And it makes sense that you'd be the last to know because I'm always the one to tell you everything." Makenzie appreciated Faith teasing her, but it was true. Makenzie would stay up half the night at their sleepovers just asking Faith questions about life and beyond. Faith was like Makenzie's Wikipedia, maybe she wasn't always right but she was closer than Makenzie on a lot of things, and she trusted her. She needed her more than anyone. "Besides, I don't know anything yet and I didn't want to upset you, I know how you'd just worry."

Makenzie took a deep breath and held the phone tightly, "So are they helping you or what, what the hell is going on?"

"Well they are giving me a bunch of pills and stuff that are supposed to help, but they don't really know what's wrong yet, so . . . I dunno. Nobody's told me what's wrong with me yet, I don't think they know, they keep taking blood and doing more tests." Faith sounded half hopeless.

"If they don't know what's wrong with you how can they give you medicine for it?" Another reason why Makenzie wished she were there to be able to ask them these questions and force some answers out of them. At the least to not let them treat Faith like she were an experiment.

"Yeah, I dunno," Faith agreed, "but guess what . . ."

"What . . . ?" Makenzie hoped Faith was going to tell her that she would be able to go home soon, that maybe the doctors would give her a call whenever they got their heads out of their asses and figured out what the hell was wrong with her instead of keeping her stuck in there on hold.

". . . I'm getting two pints of blood right now." A normal teenager would have been excited about new shoes or a new boy in school. Faith sounded excited about new blood.

"Really . . . ?" Makenzie tried not to let her words sound like "ew" and tried not to wonder whose blood she could possibly be getting or if it was a mixture of several people's blood all cleaned together.

"Yeah, it's going into me right now through an IV. They said that my heart was working too hard, that I had lost too much blood, they said I had levels of something . . . I forget what, but that it showed I had a mild heart attack . . ."

"Wow." Makenzie was stunned at the seriousness of a freaking heart attack and how much blood Faith must have lost to make her heart seize. Makenzie was worried before, but now she didn't know what to think. The Hospital wasn't a gas station, Faith couldn't just re-fuel every time she was sick and get a free hot dog and a small coffee after they punched her "pints of blood card" four times.

"Yeah it's kind of gross if you think about it, like other people's blood is going inside of me right now . . . I've got strangers' stuff inside me."

"Dude, I would have given you my blood!" Makenzie would have given anything to just get Faith better.

"I know, I love you Mazie. My mom offered too, and she was sitting right here but they said it would have taken too long. I think my mom was afraid that the blood they have here would still be wearing bell-bottoms and have AIDs or something, but they check all that stuff now."

"Yeah…I'm sure it's the best blood they have there." Makenzie tried to sound cheerful.

"You should see it though, it's kind of cool."

"Faith, you know I would love to be sitting there beside you watching your new blood with you right now. We'd sit . . . I'd paint your toenails and I'd make popcorn for you and we would just watch your new blood like a movie."

Makenzie could hear a little bit of laughter escape Faith.

"They have that here, you know, they make popcorn all the time!" Faith sounded lighter as if her hospital bed on wheels was more reminiscent of a car at a drive-in theater than a bed in a jail cell.

Makenzie wished she could be there right then making each moment less scary for Faith or at least less morbid.

She wished Faith never had to go through any of this.
She wished that whatever it was that was wrong with her would just hurry it up and fix itself.

. . . She wished for a lot of things.

Time carries itself away, with or without you.

You'd think that I had just enough time to prepare for something like this.
You'd think so.
  But time doesn't wait for anyone.
    Instead, you're the only one left waiting, for it.

. . . .

The neighborhood is still sleeping, or something like it. Me? I wouldn't know, I already forget what sleep feels like. Time used to freeze itself long enough for me to sleep at night. But I can't sleep now. The fear of something else changing keeps me awake. I can no longer trust time to be my wingman.

I lean into my dirty knees and I hug my stomach. I beg my insides not to throw up, not again, but what I'm feeling isn't nausea. This must just be what your body feels like when all of your insides are showing. When everyone can see everything about you, straight through you. There is nothing I can do now to shield myself from this vulnerability except to be where no one can see me, outside, alone.

Right then, my left hand cups over and covers my mouth and half of my nose like it's kidnapping my face. My eyes wince at the strength my non-dominant hand has. I don't know if this is happening to keep me from puking or to keep me from screaming, but I'm scared at whatever it's holding back, so I leave my hand tight across my mouth. My body is on autopilot. Perhaps indefinitely, and I nervously shake my head back and forth from behind my hand.
No, No, No . . .
Back and forth my head shakes with each no. It's the only word that comes easy now, easier than the loudest "Why" is "No."

Little jabbing pieces of driveway are indented into my skin, but I don't bother to brush them off. I have snot stains on her tank top, and her shorts are covered in dirt from me not being able to stand. I don't care.
I'll never be clean again.
Not nearly clean enough.

The air around me is quiet, the only sounds are birds starting to awake and leaves brushing each other good morning. I try to focus, for as long as I can, on the soft noises. I try to only hear the morning, but the static in my head is too loud. I can't help but listen to the noise in my head. It feels like every thought I ever had in the last eighteen years is flying through my head at the same time, at a speed that I can only grab on to one or two of them at once, but I can feel them all coming so fast. I worry if I don't pay attention to as many thoughts and memories as I can that they will all just go straight through my mind and leave forever. It feels like every thought, every feeling, and every memory that I ever had about her is rising up and escaping, quickly rushing through me like they are all still attached to her and that she is pulling them behind her, and that they too will be gone forever.

I can't lose them too.

So I try to hold on to as many as I can. Even the most simple, stupid memories are coming up to the surface and it's too much. It hurts to have them flooded through me right now. I wonder where they are all coming from inside me that it hurts so deeply. It feels like all these collected years were holding me together and now as each memory comes up and escapes it's unraveling me and I can feel the pain of a thousand stitches of time unraveling at once.

Each memory that surfaces leaves behind more emptiness. Replays of conversations strike holes in my heart.

Then I realize, as I'm looking at each moment closer, that none of these memories are the same. I wish she were here and I'd ask her if she remembered them this new way too. But she's not here to verify any of them. At all.

Even the most cherished memories are not what they were a few days ago. They hold so much pain now, and it makes me wish they never even came up. If only I could have saved them from this blanket of pain and kept them precious and perfect forever.

Now, though, they are tainted. Now all of these memories are coming up, rising up to be re-filed under "pain." And the worst thing about this new painful filing system is that every old feeling and memory has a new date. Instead of 'last Christmas', or the 'spring of Junior Prom', or the 'best summer ever,' instead of memories of our sleepovers and our road trips, now every memory is stamped with a new time reference and it's stamped with:

"Never Again." All of them have this coating and I can't un-do it.

I'm feeling dizzy again.

More tears fall as I mourn the memories themselves. I knew this would change the future, I knew it would make everything ahead harder, but I didn't realize until now that it would change the past too. All of it. Nothing goes untouched. And I feel like nothing up to this point has been real. Has it? I don't know because she's not here to tell me, she's not here to defend the amount of memories I have that only have *her* in them. It feels like she is the only witness to half of my life and without her I barely even exist. There's no proof. Without her, I will have to explain to people who I am and where I've been, without any proof.

I stay on the ground while the sun rises higher along with the failure in me and I wonder how I could have better prepared for this. I wonder how anyone can ever prepare for the worst moment of their life.

But no one can.

Because *Time* is like a *Disease*.

It has spread from being the worst moment of my life, into the worst day of my life, into the complete annihilation of the rest of my life.

And there is no cure

Except . . .

    More time.

        Ironic isn't it.

I have nothing to do but wait.

So I sit.

And I sit.

And I know that someone will come out to get me soon, to check on me, to ask me if I'm "okay." And I already know what I will tell them, I will say *"I'm Fine."* I'm the furthest thing from "fine," but it's what they want to hear.

There is no other answer.

There is no telling people that I'm not okay because I cannot fall apart. I'm fine.

If they don't believe me, then they'll sit down next to me, or reach for me. They will try and touch me and I won't mean to but I'll lean away from them. They won't understand but it will hurt even worse to feel anything else but this pain inside me. Any touch will burn through my skin into my heart and only remind me again of what is really happening. Any touch at all will resemble a burning pinch that I desperately need to wake up, but I won't. Because this isn't a dream.

If my leaning away doesn't give them a clue, they will then ask if I need someone to talk to. *Like I could talk about any of this right now, or ever.* As if my feelings could even form human words. So I will just shake my head "no" because any more words that come out of my mouth right now won't sound like my own. And I can't stand to hear the pain in my own voice. It's a stranger. Everything is so strange.

And then, if they are still there after all of that rejection, what they'll do last is ask what they really wanted to know first.

"What happened that day?"

And I just might be able to tell them about the moment that I will be stuck in forever.

But I won't.

I can't.

Because it doesn't matter what happened. The fact that it happened made it the worst possible thing. There's these people that just think it's conversation to ask, like it's the details that make this story. It's not the details that make this real. She's gone, and the last thing that ever happened to her is my least favorite thing to think about. I'm over the courtesies of conversation about it, because I know what they will say if I do tell them.

They will all say the same fucking thing,
"Time will heal all wounds."
And I can't hear that now.
Because Time doesn't erase things.

And it certainly doesn't bring them back . . .

Makenzie

"Hello?" As soon as Faith picked up the receiver, Makenzie could hear the beeping of the Hospital through the phone.

"Hey, best friend!" Makenzie tried to sound extra cheery and cheesy.

"Hey, Mazie . . ." Faith just sounded exhausted, still.

"So how are you feeling, man? Are you feeling any better?" Makenzie asked over the phone trying not to picture Faith in one of those hospital gowns with the little ties in the back that really tie around to the side. The ones that are really only made like that to make it easier to undress sick people when they're dead in the morgue. Makenzie tried not to think about the morgue of the hospital.

"Eh . . . I'm fine." Faith's voice wasn't as faint as it was the last time they spoke but it still wasn't how Makenzie wanted her to sound.

"Fay. You're not fine. Okay. You're in the fucking Hospital, you don't need to tell me that. You can tell other people that you're fine, but me, I want to hear how you are really feeling."

"I'm Fiiiiine." Faith's words drew out like they were traveling with an eye roll.

"Fay, people don't go to the Hospital when they are '*fine*'." Makenzie shook her head and waved her hand in the air in front of her as if Faith would be able to see her dramatics through the phone. "The kids I saw at my school today, yeah, they are all fine. Some of them, maybe a little mental, but fine. But you, you didn't go to your school today, did you Fay? Because you're in the Hospital!"

"Fine, I'm 'okay'. I'm tired most of the time, but they let me sleep here whenever I want. And I haven't had any attacks lately, probably because I'm mostly lying down, but I'm okay . . . I'm gonna be okay." Faith sounded unconvincing. Makenzie was glad to hear that she at least wasn't having any more of what Faith called "attacks." She didn't know what they were but the ones that Makenzie had witnessed were sudden and scary. The last time it happened they were at the mall, in a store, just talking by a rack of clothes and Faith's face went blank right before she dropped to her knees. She was crunched down just holding her stomach and couldn't even talk to tell Makenzie what was happening, she could only unblinkingly hold her breath until it passed. Makenzie remembers bending down to be with Faith, waiting there with her and holding her other hand, using her own body as an orange cone for people to go around and not walk near Faith while it was happening. When it was over, Faith would just shake her head and say quietly how she hated it when that happened. She would brush off those blasts of pain shooting through her abdomen so hard that it brought her to her knees like it was normal. It left her sweating.

It wasn't normal.

"Well that's good, I'm glad you're resting. And you know you don't have to lie to me, Fay, you can tell me how it really is, and you don't have to pretend with me . . ." Makenzie felt like reminding Faith that she knew way before her that Santa Claus was not a real gig.

"I know . . . I wasn't scared you know . . ."

Makenzie had just convinced her to open up, that she could take hearing anything, but she immediately felt wrong. She didn't want to hear what it sounded like Faith was about to say next . . .

"Fay. Don't talk like that. You're going to be OKAY. You're going to be okay and there's nothing to be afraid of."

"I know, that's what I'm saying—I'm not afraid to die." Faith said those words cheerier than any Makenzie had heard her say in a long time.

How could she say it like that? Makenzie couldn't find words. She didn't know how to say that she wanted her to be afraid to die so that she wouldn't give up. She didn't know how to tell her that she was afraid of her dying.

Faith filled the silence, "I just don't know . . . I guess . . . what I'm supposed . . . to do next . . ."

"What do you mean?" Makenzie wanted to grab Faith by the shoulders, "Ya just live, Fay!" Makenzie felt something in her stomach that reminded her of disgust, and the very word she hated Faith using was now the same one she would force on to her, "You're gonna be FINE, Fay!" and she hoped it were true, "You're going to be just *fine*."

She needed Faith to be fine.

She needed her more than anything.

Faith

Most people don't know the exact day or moment that changes their lives. But people that are in hospitals are constantly waiting for this moment, hoping it closer or further away.

Faith had waited for months to hear what the doctors would say. Every time she met a new white lab coat, she would prepare for it. She would think, *this is it*. She had spent too much time preparing for the worst. Faith had Googled her symptoms. She web-md-ed them. She knew what the possibilities were. The whole world has cancer, dormant cancer cells floating and clinging inside them that just aren't alive yet. Why not her?
Why shouldn't the only thing alive in her be death?

When the Doctor came in that day, Faith wasn't thinking about anything. She wasn't thinking about what other kids her age in school were doing right then. This was her life now. She was ready. And she reminded herself as he was finding the chair in front of her moveable bed, that he couldn't hurt her any worse than what she had already been through.
Whatever he was going to say could only bring relief. One way or another, she would finally know everything. The one thing that ascends beyond feeling good or feeling bad is just feeling the truth. She would finally know what was wrong with her and could stop worrying about the unknown. The unknown could be a million things. The truth could only be one. Maybe just by knowing, her load could get a little lighter.

When the Doctor sat down, he didn't have any small talk. They never do. That was okay. No need to belittle the situation.
He had told Faith and her mom what they had heard before and what every person who has to go through any amount of tests and scans and procedures usually hears as the preface: "Well we don't know yet for certain," and then came words that held unusual hope,
"But we have it narrowed down . . ."

He had named two things. It was either one or the other.
Two things Faith had never heard of before.
Two things that were diseases
Two things that he explained, were incurable.
> Ulcerative Colitis.
> Or Crohn's Disease.

Faith didn't know which one to hope that she had.
Tears were screaming to be let out from behind her eyes.
Her hands hugged her stomach.

She didn't want either of them.
She never wanted any of this.

Makenzie

She walked as fast as she could home from school. Her feet hit the concrete below her with thuds that shook her whole body. Her backpack jumped up and down on her lower back with each step. When the sidewalk ran out, she walked with large strides on the side of the road. Each car that passed drove close enough that she could feel the whoosh of recycled air run over her face.

She looked ahead at the traffic light that had just turned yellow and she counted the number of cars that blew through it.

Three.

She focused on the car that was stopped, and she wondered if he were thinking about how he was sure to be stuck at a red light for the next four lights on the stretch of highway.

Because that's the thing about yellow lights.

They are meant to slow everyone down.

But if cars go through enough of them, they'll be seeing green again. That fourth car should have just gone for it. They could have made it.

Makenzie started to run, well knowing that she could never slow herself down, even when told to.

She ran past each car that had just blown by her and imagined pushing the same amount of air against them as they had brushed by her with. And as the light turned green, she turned the corner to the hill of houses down her street.

She arrived at her house and looked up at her bedroom window from the sidewalk. She opened the back gate and walked through the back door through the kitchen and went straight up to her room. She didn't even look in the refrigerator or sniff the air for possible signs of dinner. She just wanted to call Faith.

She had waited all day to know if today was the day they would tell Faith when she was going home. She threw her door open and slid her backpack into the corner. She picked up the phone and dialed the numbers that she had already memorized.

She counted the rings.

Eight.

And she hung up and dialed again, carefully consulting the yellow sticky note with Faith's hospital phone number and extension stuck next to the phone. She probably just missed a number.

She waited and counted the rings.

Eight.

Nothing.

At all.

She quickly dialed Faith's cell phone and waited.
Straight to voicemail.
{Fuck.}

Makenzie took a deep breath and tried to keep fears silenced. She told herself *not to think about it.* Maybe Faith was just in the bathroom, or down the hall, or maybe they were discharging her. Yes, that was it. Don't think about anything else, she thought.

She dialed 411 and asked for the hospital's main line. She would call every phone number that the hospital had to get hold of her if she had to. The 411 operator didn't understand the rush of Makenzie's words and had to ask again which hospital she was trying to reach. Makenzie slowed her speech and the operator transferred her to the Hospital's information desk. Three rings and then Makenzie told them "I need to know if room 704 is still Faith Hayward?"

The front desk lady put Makenzie through five whole seconds of listening to her breathe while she checked the computer, before Makenzie was sure that Faith was still breathing.

"Yes, that is the patient in 704."

Confirmed.

At least they didn't move her somewhere.

And Makenzie tried not to think about where it is that they would have moved her to.

Faith

She lay in the same position she had for the last week, but now, even that wasn't good enough. A Nurse had come to invite her to some activity down the hall, and when she declined, the Nurse had said that it was okay if she didn't feel like it today but that tomorrow she would have to at least walk her IV machine up and down the hall to start exercising her muscles.

Last week they didn't want her to do more than eat and go to the bathroom. Days before that she wasn't even allowed to eat. And now, now that she has a disease, she has to get up and "exercise"?

And that was how it was going to be. There was always going to be someone there to tell her what to do, what to eat, and what to feel. She would never have control of her own life again, because even when these people stopped telling her these things, the disease inside her would control her. She didn't need a doctor to tell her that this disease would now run and ruin her life. She already knew it.

She hated the term that they had for the disease living inside of her. Instead of being in classes at school right then, she was now in a class of diseases. An Autoimmune Disease. It made it sound like her life would be on autopilot in the wrong direction forever. Sometimes she would hear the doctors and nurses call it an autoimmune disorder. A disorder. Like it was no big deal. Like she just had a touch of A.D.D. or something that practically everyone had. Like an autoimmune disorder was the type of disease that wasn't so bad because it's not like cancer cells that take over and eat away at your body.

No, an autoimmune disease was just her own organs eating away at themselves.

Cancer wasn't the enemy. *She was* the enemy.

As if she couldn't feel any more let down and given up on, her own body was now eating away at itself. Faith's immune system, the very thing inside of her that was supposed to always protect her, fight for her, and never leave her, had decided that it was just over her.

She could feel her stomach moving inside itself as if it knew she was outraged about it. She hated that thing inside of her so much. And somehow giving it a name gave it more power. It now had a proper title, like the disease inside her had just been knighted. Faith wished that her organs could have worn armor to protect themselves. Her only weapons were her fists, and her right hand halfheartedly punched herself right in the side, and she started to cry.

The phone next to her bed rang and the little light on top of it blinked bright red. She reached for the phone, stretching the IV cord attached to her hand to a length that made it pinch, and she slid the short black knob on the side of the receiver to "OFF."

She couldn't answer the phone.
She had enough answers for one day.

Makenzie

The sun moved into her eyes but she had been awake for hours. She didn't sleep well wondering where Faith was last night that she didn't answer the phone all of the times she had called. She had called the front desk two more times to see if they could tell her anything else. And despite how hard she tried not to think about it, she couldn't help that one thought from popping in.

What if something happened to Faith and she was the last to know.
She couldn't imagine what she would do without her.
She hated thinking about that.

She needed to see her. Makenzie wished more than anything that night that she could have just picked up a pair of keys and driven a car to the hospital, she didn't care that the hospital was an hour and a half away, she would have been there every day. She would have given her left ass cheek to be able to drive. But being fifteen was a handicap in life; not only could Makenzie not drive, but she could barely steer life in her direction. She couldn't control her own life or control anything that was happening around her.
She hated it.
She just needed Faith to be okay.

Faith

She tolerated being poked, squeezed, and pumped with needles and medicine every day. But what she dreaded most about the nurses' visits wasn't that they took so much blood that they needed a little plastic square basket to transport all the vials in like freaking Red Riding Hood with her picnic basket, or the fact that they would press their hospital cold hands all over her stomach trying to reach deep enough to touch her back asking *"does that hurt?"* What she hated the most were the conversations that they all tried to have with her while they did those things. They'd ask her the same questions about how she was doing, or ask about her family, as if something had dramatically changed for the better in her health or her relationship status since yesterday. Some of the nurses would ask her if she had any pets, and she told one of them she had a dog. And when they asked her the follow-up question that everyone gets with dogs, *"Oh yeah? What kind of dog?"* Faith had said, *"I dunno, just a regular dog, okay?"*

She didn't have a dog.

But she was just so tired of them prodding her for information about her life as if her life before this was fucking glamorous and it would bring up great memories to distract her from being in the Hospital.

They didn't for a second think that maybe being in the Hospital now was a needed distraction from the rest of her life.

Because no one would guess that about anyone.

{But it was true.}

Faith hated the cheery daytime nurses. She slept through as much of the day as she could and waited for the night shift nurses.

The night nurses were her favorite.

And not just because they didn't talk as much.

But because when they did talk, it was comforting.

They would come in for the round the clock check-ins and medicines and before they did anything they would all say the same thing,

"It's okay, I'm just checking your blood pressure."

"It's okay, I'm just changing your IV fluid."

"It's okay, I'm just giving you another steroid drip."

Whatever the night nurse would say at 2 am would always start with *"It's okay . . ."* and Faith would roll over and open her eyes when they came in on cue, just to hear them say,

"It's okay, you can go back to sleep now . . ."

Because sometimes that's all anyone needs to hear in order to heal.
Even when it's 2 am.
Even when it's a stranger telling you.
Even when it's worlds away from ever being "okay" again.

Makenzie

The front door to her house was locked. Christ on a cracker. She was always locked out. She banged her fist three times quickly on her own front door but something about her being locked out didn't make it feel like hers. She waited for only a second before backtracking and breaking in through the back gate. She wouldn't have even tried the front door had she not seen her dad's Audi in the driveway. She might have felt like she actually belonged there if they would have given her a house key. Or better yet picked her up from school so that she wouldn't need to find her own way home or walk so far. Or maybe just be mildly anticipating her to arrive home at the same time every day and show it via an unlocked door.

She headed upstairs to her room and on her way saw her dad on his laptop doing work in the living room. She asked him jokingly, but seriously, "Why is the front door always locked even when you're home?"

And he said "Makenzie, please." As if that were an answer.

She trekked the stairs, and when she reached her room she closed the door behind her and let out a sigh that she felt like she had been holding on to all day. She picked up the phone and dialed ten numbers that meant nothing to her weeks ago.

Two rings. She heard the release of the receiver and smiled.

". . . Hello?"

"FAY!" Makenzie whisper-screamed, so thankful that Faith was there.

"Hey, Mazie, how was school . . . ?" Faith asked in a way that Makenzie imagined only mothers did, asking about school days before any new business was discussed. The kind of thing most kids probably think is so beyond annoying. And maybe it would be annoying if Makenzie had been asked it every day, or some days, but she wasn't ever asked how her day was, at all. Only by Faith. And she couldn't stand to think for a second that she might lose that.

"Dude. Where *were* you yesterday! I tried calling your room all night!" Makenzie had imagined yelling at Faith for being MIA and to never do that again to her, but could only elevate her voice to 'concerned'.

"Oh sorry, yeah I turned this room phone off."

"Fay. Don't you ever do that again! I freaked on the front desk people looking for you."

"What? You called downstairs?"

"Yes, I was worried about you!" Makenzie didn't know how many times she would have to say it before Faith knew what that meant.

"Mazie, you don't have to worry," Faith exhaled, "I'm not going . . . anywhere." But Faith said it in a way that sounded like she wished she were. Makenzie hated that.

She couldn't stand thinking about Faith leaving her.

Breathe in deeply.
And you'll notice your own breath in a way that you never have before.
    The sound it makes.
        The push it creates on your body.

        At first you'll notice it because you've never had to try this hard just to keep breathing. But you'll keep noticing it, because every breath will bounce off your heartbeat, echoing that you're alive.

. . . .

    I sit quietly outside with the stillness of the sun that has risen. The morning has arrived and the day has come. And I brace myself for the world to go on without her. I sit in a ball in the driveway and I wait for neighbors to rush out of the surrounding houses with hands full of coffee and keys, and high heels that say "I'm late, I'm late" with every step. But I wait, and I wait, and it seems that even strangers are letting me down today.

    The whole world has let me down.

    Maybe it's too early.

    Maybe it's a weekend.

    And I search in a back-up drive of my memory to try to recall what day it is. But I can't find it. It's like everything really is gone.

I can only tell what day it is in relation to one thing:

    It's Day One Without Her.

    And I wonder if I will only ever be able to measure things in reference to having her or not having her. I wonder if anything that used to matter, like the time on the clock, the day or the week, or the seasons in the sky, I wonder if all of these universal measurements will ever matter to me again. Or if I'll always feel like the rest of my life is just one big long bad day, one big chunk of time that's just to be measured as: "without her."

    Over the loud silence and the screaming feelings, there is this voice inside of my head that keeps showing up, and it's saying "*you have no idea how hard this is going to be.*" And that's an honest voice.

    Because I really don't know,
                  at all.

I know it will be hard, it's already so hard to just breathe, but I don't know when I will comprehend the gravity of this. Right now, part of me still doesn't believe that this is real. So much of this new reality is spent thinking about the past and thinking about the future, and this present is just . . . lacking. While stuck in this unwelcomed sequence of moments, my entire being is saying "NO, this can't be."

And I hate that thought, because every time I feel it, it encourages the argumentative side of my brain to validate and prove the authenticity of these moments. And then I'm led to feeling the worst disloyalty ever as internal parts of me provide proof that she is actually gone. And if any ounce of me is still fighting this reality, then my brain brings up the most painful, hurtful word it can find; without apologizing, without letting me down easy, my brain lashes out with reality and says, *"She's dead."*

And I hate myself for thinking those words.

But I need to keep reminding myself of it. That this is how it is now. It's so painful to have to remind myself that this is the truth. But I need to learn that this is how my days will feel, what they will look like, and what they will be filled with. And that no matter how much I choose not to believe it, it is still in fact happening. It won't stop happening.

There's so much I'm trying to digest about this.

And all I want to do, more than anything, is throw up.

Faith

There were heavy footsteps at her door but no knock.

A little boy walked through her doorway and Faith looked at him as if he were a barium milkshake in a Styrofoam drink container.

He introduced himself like any eight-year-old would, except he had to pull down a hospital mask to talk. He asked Faith her name and before she could even respond, he asked quickly if she wanted to play a board game with him.

Faith looked to the door behind the boy, wishing that Hospital Security was on the lookout for him and would just usher him along to where he belonged already.

He moved closer and closer to her bed as he talked and when she still didn't answer, he listed each game that the Hospital child's wing had. The little boy wore blue jeans and a red and white striped T-shirt, and if he hadn't had the recognizable hospital bracelet and the mask over his face, Faith might have wondered what he was doing in the Children's Hospital.

Faith said, "That's okay," to decline the game invitation but the little boy just repeated the Hospital's selection of board games. Faith shook her head and creased her eyebrows down at him before looking away to the tv hanging on the wall that had been on the same channel for days. Maybe if she just didn't make eye contact again, he would go away.

But with the attitude of someone ten years older, the boy asked her, "What else are you going to do, watch Maury Povich all day?"

He was right. She was trapped. And she already knew who all the fathers were on the paternity tests because the noon showing was just a repeat from yesterday's four o'clock episode.

So she said "Connect Four."

And he offered to go get the game himself before running out the door.

Faith couldn't move anyways.

It took her the whole time the boy was gone to sit up in her bed and cross her bare naked legs underneath the sheets. Just from sitting up she could feel how much her back hurt, and she started to rub her lower left side before she remembered that her whole body hurt and that she didn't care. Faith fixed the blankets and hoped that the little boy knew that she wouldn't be leaving those covers. She didn't have the luxury of wearing clothes like him; all she had to wear was an oversized bib and a pair of underwear.

She looked at the clock, and she looked at Maury. And she thought maybe it wouldn't be so bad to talk to someone she didn't know about things that didn't matter for a while, even if he were just a kid. Because at least he wouldn't know what was wrong with her. And she hoped he wouldn't ask. She wondered if hospitals were like jails in the sense that it was some kind of unspoken rule not to ask others what they were in for or when they were getting out. Because she didn't want to talk about it. And she didn't want anyone just looking at her wondering what she did so wrong to end up there.

The boy came back in the room with two games and Faith took a deep breath. She wasn't playing whatever the second one was. She'd play Connect Four, it was short and it would be over quickly and the little boy would be back on his way. As the boy unpacked the board and explained to Faith the rules of Connect Four, as if the name didn't imply enough, Faith could see a smile spread over his cheeks from under his mask. Maybe she'd play him the best two out of three.

And with his muffled words about picking colors and who would go first, she wondered why he had to wear a mask.

Was that to protect him, or to protect other people from him?

Should she be wearing a mask?

What if what he had was contagious?

The little boy pulled the mask away from his face and shifted it to rest on his neck, and like all little kids that try to make you feel more comfortable by saying something awkward and obvious, he simply looked at Faith to answer her stares and said,

"Sometimes, I throw up blood, that's why I wear this. But just sometimes."

And then Faith felt bad.

She felt bad about everything.

Makenzie

She stood beside her Grandma in the yellow and blue kitchen and watched her chop vegetables for Sunday's family dinner. At noon tomorrow everyone would be sitting around that table in tall wooden-backed chairs like they did every week, everyone except for Faith. It wasn't right. Nothing felt right anymore.

Makenzie leaned in and asked her Grandma, "Will Faith be okay . . . ?" as if her Grandmother were operating on Faith right then and not julienning carrots. Makenzie's elbows pressed against the kitchen counter's hard surface.

"Of course she will." Her Grandma said with eyes that only grandmas have, and she turned from the carrots and picked up potatoes to start peeling them into the sink. Makenzie wished she could have believed her Grandma as much as she really wanted to.

But she didn't.

She didn't believe any of this was really happening.

Makenzie raised her voice over the water running over potatoes. "And why do I need to go to church tomorrow with Grandpa to pray to a God for her to get better when God is the reason that she is sick." And like the sink, Makenzie's eyes were filling up with water. "How can there be a God if he lets things like this happen? Why are there so many sick kids that they need separate hospitals just to fit them all in? Is God on vacation right now?"

Makenzie wiped her eyes, upset that she was crying and taking it out on Grandma as if she made the rules, "It's not fair!"

And her Grandmother said "I know," and did what not all Grandmas can do. She put down what she was doing and gave Makenzie a hug so tight that it felt like it was the only thing holding Makenzie together. And Makenzie let out all her tears at once, because sometimes one good hug could do that. And Makenzie said, "Faith's going to be okay, she has to be," and she pleaded in a way that almost made it true.

Her Grandma pulled back from the hug and reassured her, by nodding slowly and surely, "Faith will get better and come home soon," and her Grandma leaned back in and wrapped arms around Makenzie again, pressing Makenzie's head against her chest in a hug so big that Makenzie had to close her eyes and only hear the words that her Grandmother was saying as she continued, "Because you girls are strong." And her Grandma squeezed her again, "You girls can get through anything." Makenzie could feel her Grandma nodding, as her head brushed above hers when she spoke, "You two are survivors."

Faith

She sat up in bed and felt out of place. To her, anything that wasn't lying down felt like she had annoyingly accomplished something that day.

The doctor had told Faith's mom that she could bring Faith pajamas to wear, and her mom had brought her in some the very next day. Faith thought about how good it felt to have substantial fabric hugging close to her bare legs and ran her fingernails over the fuzzy texture of her blue pajama bottoms. She admired her new comfort for only a minute before, like an idiot, she realized what those clothes meant.

As much as she unloved the thin diamond-patterned-off-the-shoulder piece she had worn for the last week straight, the thing that they called a gown even though it was most certainly not a gown in any definition of the glamorous word. The word "gown" was as un-fitting as the fabric itself. As much as she hated the gown, it allowed her to believe that she would only be there for one more day. It was always the plan, in her mind, to leave the next morning.

But not anymore.

Because she had unknowingly signed a contract of her willingness to stay in the Hospital the second she slid both legs into those pajama bottoms. And now she was defeated—again. Her eyes winced and she looked away from her pants around the room. She was wearing her clothes in the Hospital, just like the little boy.

The boy that had to wear a mask because he coughed up blood.

The boy that all the nurses on the seventh floor called by name as he ran by.

The boy that said it was his third time visiting the Hospital like he were talking about a vacation spot and held up three fingers on one hand proudly as if it were his age.

That boy.

Her entire body felt like it was nodding her head. It all made sense in a really shitty way. She wouldn't be leaving the Hospital that day, or the next, or the one after that. Because in a Hospital there are only two kinds of patients:

Ones that came in frantic on a Friday and were home before Monday even crossed their mind. A man with a crippling power tool injury, a little boy with a broken arm simply from being a little boy, a pregnant mother who shocked herself by accident getting a piece of late night toast; these people took priority on the lowest level on the Hospital. They rarely had to visit any other Hospital floor than "G" or "star" if it wasn't to get some sort of scan or X-ray.

Get them in.
Fix them.
And get them back on their way.
That was their "treatment plan."

And then there were the other ones. The ones that may have started their visits as an assumed emergency but who have now worked their way up the Hospital floor ladder. These were the ones that were there to stay. These were the people that kept the Hospital gift shops profitable. And these were the people the Hospital chapels were built for. They kept the cafeteria busy with their daily menu requests for breakfast, lunch, and dinner. They were the stayers. They came to the Hospital and felt like they were at home.

Faith wasn't just there to get tests anymore. She was one of the stayers now. She wasn't an emergency, she was a patient. And she already knew that the chicken fingers were the best thing on the menu because she had tried everything else. And this was going to be her life.
Hospital visits and tests.
Taking medicine and being sick.
She never wanted that.
This couldn't be her life.

But the blue-patterned fuzz on her comfortable pajama pants screamed differently. Faith looked around the room, trying to imagine the Hospital room as the living room setting of the rest of her life. The blood pressure machine next to her was tall and loud like a grandfather clock, squeezing her arm and beeping every hour on the hour. She didn't want this to be her life, but it already was.

Faith wished the little boy in the red and white striped shirt, jeans, and a mask could have been there right then so she could have asked him something. Or just sat with him. Maybe even played another stupid game.

She felt so unprepared for her Hospital initiation. Everything in the little pale yellow Hospital room now reminded her of the little boy leaving and his last set of words before he put the white fabric tent back over his mouth. She had asked him how long he had been at the Hospital and he said, *"I'm only here to get more medicine"* as he skipped out of her doorway. And like a child Faith asked a one-word question and expected a lifetime of answers, *"Why?"* And the way he looked at her, the smirk his eyes gave her above the mask laughed at her as if she was pulling his leg, like she really knew the answer but was just making sure that he knew.

But she didn't know.
She didn't know at all.
"Because, you always have to get new medicines!" He said it like he was amused at her silly question. Like getting new medicines was the same practice as buying new shoes every year before school started.
New medicine. . .

Thinking about the disease growing, and changing so much, scared her. What would happen to her body that made the medicine stop working? Faith wished that she didn't have so many new questions.

. . . She wished for a lot of things.

Makenzie

The elevator stopped on floors 2, 3, and 6, and so did Makenzie's heart. She couldn't wait to see Faith, but thinking about her in a hospital bed made her stomach vibrate through her body, and the heavy jerking elevator gears on the journey didn't help.

The elevator doors opened and welcomed Makenzie, her grandparents, and her friend from church onto the seventh floor. Makenzie and the girl with the cross around her neck had spent their entire Sunday School class dodging lessons about Jesus and instead making Get Well cards for Faith. They even looted the classrooms of the younger kids for the best crayons. Makenzie knew that Jesus would understand. He's been through some shit, after all, and Makenzie was sure that if she knew Jesus at all that he would have loved a freaking handmade Get Well card when he was on the cross.

Makenzie realized how tightly her hand was holding on to her homemade card, and she looked down to see that she had creased it with anticipation. Makenzie tried to straighten it out while quickly trying to figure out which way to go from the elevator.

The Hospital was filled with paper everywhere. On the walls were folders, charts, signs telling about fire exits, directories for room numbers, and maps for cafeterias. There were posters up on the wall, glossy oversized prints advertising medicine, or disease—Makenzie couldn't tell which they were promoting. Makenzie frantically searched for a sign that said "Faith—this way—>;" there wasn't one, but there should have been. They followed the little room number arrows from directory plaques: 700–724, right. Makenzie walked swiftly ahead of her grandparents and her friend and took long strides past open doorways, past the rooms that were numbered like houses. Once she reached 704, she stopped for just a second, unsure if that was really the right room. She thought it might feel different than the other rooms she had just passed with beeping machines and stale tv sounds coming out of them, but it didn't. It had the same dead air and hospital smell coming from the doorway.

Makenzie entered the room, and saw Faith. It was the right room, but it was all wrong. Faith had an ugly white blanket draped over her and Makenzie could see the exact outline of her bones through it. Faith's eyes had small green rings around dime-size black pupils. Her forehead had more wrinkles creased into it than Makenzie had ever seen. All in all, she looked far more dead than alive and Makenzie questioned in her mind if the tubes and wires going into Faith were really to help her, or were they doing the opposite and sucking the life right out of her? What was Faith in there for if she wasn't getting better?

Makenzie walked past a corkboard on the wall with scattered pamphlets, newsletters, and a laminated chart of smiley faces. By the look on Faith's face, Makenzie wondered if that chart was for Faith to practice smiling every day like some kind of weird re-hab. She looked miserable. And Makenzie let out a "Hiiii" with her voice waving like her arms as if Faith were the guest of honor at a surprise party. Makenzie wished she could have just ran up to Faith and bounced on the hospital bed to give her a hug, but it looked like even sitting next to her gently would have hurt Faith.

Faith's grandparents lined up to hug her; Makenzie waited until the girl with the cross around her neck gave her a hug before handing Faith the homemade Get Well card and giving her a light squeeze.

They all filtered into the room and sat in wide-armed wooden chairs around Faith's bed. The chairs below their butts were worse than the wooden pews they had just come from, but the awkwardness in the room masked the hardness on Makenzie's bottom.

They all sat, looking at Faith, trying to hold smiles.

Faith asked, "What are you doing here . . ." in a tone that made Makenzie hate those words. Faith said them as if her family were an ex-boyfriend at some stupid high school party.

"What do you mean '*what are we doing here*,' we came to see you," Makenzie forced the biggest smile she had, but was afraid that she may be showing too many teeth.

"Oh, thanks," Faith mumbled, un-phased by the surprise visit or the get well wishes.

Faith had wires coming out of her from every direction and Makenzie couldn't keep from trying to trace them with her eyes to see where they could all possibly be going. Makenzie thought with so many things hooked up and going into her that she should look better, fuller. But Faith looked deflated. And with all of the white around Faith, Makenzie thought she should have looked fresh, but instead she looked like she was wasting away. Nothing about any of this made sense. Makenzie tried not to show on her face what she was really thinking, she tried to smile as Grandma sat down beside Faith's bed and asked, "So, how are you feeling?"

And Faith said, "I'm Fine."
    Makenzie knew she wasn't.
        Nothing was fine.

Faith

The nurses didn't know when Faith would be discharged, but they all made it sound like it would be soon. So every day she hoped they would surprise her with the official "treatment plan," some sort of welcome to your new life packet, and then get her on her merry way.

But every day she ended up just waiting herself into a coma of depression.

The doctors even talked about sending her home with a traveling IV to keep steroids running straight through her rather than pills. But with all the talk about sending her home with this they never once alluded to when exactly that would be.

Faith couldn't take the feeling of not knowing again, and asked the next Nurse that came in with a round of pills, "What's the deal, when can I go home?"

It was a young male Nurse who was trying to cheer her up with his answer without revealing too much information, "The good news is that you aren't getting any worse," as if it could get worse. He had no idea. "But they can't discharge you until you're a little healthier," he said while switching out an empty IV bag for a full one. Faith didn't realize that there were tiers of "healthy" with a disease and she asked him what that meant,

"What do you mean healthier, I'm going to be sick forever."

He pressed a few buttons on her tall clunky blood pressure machine and heart monitor screen and explained, "Well, legally the Hospital can't send anyone home who's bleeding. We just wouldn't be doing our job then. Like... Say, if you came in with a big cut on the outside of your skin and needed stiches, we wouldn't send you home till you got patched up and we stopped the bleeding, it's the same for your insides."

Faith was annoyed. It all came down to the blood. And she couldn't stop the bleeding. She had been bleeding out her insides for the last two months straight, and what if that didn't change? Her insides were bleeding because her organs were attacking themselves, it wasn't anything they could just stitch up.

"What if it takes forever, I really have to stay here that long?" Faith whined for the first time out loud. The male Nurse re-assured her, "The medicine should help soon, and the other thing they are watching is your weight."

"Oh . . ." Faith looked confused; she never thought about her weight.

"Since you only weighed ninety-six pounds when you came in, it's how we will know that the steroids are working. The steroids will make you gain weight when they are doing their job. I think once you reach one hundred pounds, even if you're still bleeding, the doctors will feel better about sending you home with the steroids kicking in."

So it came down to four pounds. If she was four pounds heavier she would be four pounds healthier, and maybe even four pounds happier.

Maybe.

Our lives are filled with "Firsts" that get bigger as you get older.
        First bike.
                First kiss.
                        First car . . .

But what nobody tells you, is that death has its own "firsts."

        And they won't tell you that when you lose someone you love, these firsts will take over your whole life. And almost all of them, will hurt like hell.

        You'll spend all of your time counting death's firsts and collecting them in hopes that the more you have, the closer you will be to that one day when you see them again.

. . . .

And when it feels like I've been alone outside defeated by daylight forever, someone from inside the house that isn't mine is awake and comes out to look for me. They come walking towards me, sleep in their eyes, and they ask me if I need anything. My instinct is to shake my head, and my only thought is about how much I need her.

But something important breaks though, and I nod.

And I mumble, ". . . A notebook."

They look confused, as if I'm referencing some sort of secret notebook that we will need a map to unearth, or some magic notebook that holds the blueprints of a time machine that will help us go back and undo all of this.

But all I need is a plain regular notebook.

And I say it again, because they look lost, "Just a regular lined notebook . . ."

And they say, "Of course, I'll get you one right away." But I can tell that they are still confused, afraid that they'll go to the store and not get the right kind.

Because suddenly everyone is afraid of disappointing me.

They all just want so badly to make me happy.

But what they don't understand is that I can be neither of those things.

Not right now, or maybe ever again.

My thoughts rest now on the idea of the notebook. I need it. I just need to write to her, wherever she is, and tell her all of these things that are happening, or just save them in ink so that I remember to tell her when I see her again. I'm choked by the thought of having to hold on to any words, or thoughts, or feelings until I see her again. Unimportant chatter that only she would understand grabs on to my throat with two hands.

I need to put these words somewhere.

I need to tell her.

I need her to know that she was right. She was always right.

And she'll know. But we need to laugh about it. The kind of seconds-right-after-something-bad-happens-and-she-could-make-me-laugh-about-anything moment. I want to tell her every stupid thing that's happened since yesterday but I want to tell her in a way that she would be on the floor laughing at all of this.

I want to make her feel better about it.

I want to tell her that it's okay.

The only way I know how to do that is to make her laugh again.

And I try to think about all of the times that we laughed so hard that we cried.

And I don't know why I'm craving laughter so badly right now. It's the furthest from what I'm actually feeling. My eyes are swollen and my face is bloated from crying. My cheeks are raw from the constant salt of tears. But in my everlasting sadness, I just want to hear her laugh.

And in my core, I know that she's already smiling. Somewhere she is healthy and flowing, lightweight and airy, and smiling the biggest fucking smile that I may never see again, but as long as she's smiling.

And I know that she is.

She has to be.

Because it's all over now.

The fight is over.

Faith

The first time Faith had ever come home from a Hospital, it was two days after she was born, fifteen years ago, and it was on a June summer's day—Father's Day.

This second time that she came home from the Hospital, was almost late fall, everything around her was dying and her father was gone for good.

The exact moment that Faith knew her dad really wasn't going to come back was the exact same moment that she told Makenzie that he had left. The thing that she had feared the most would happen, did: As soon as the words came out of her mouth, he was really gone.

Faith was at her Grandma's house, and even though she knew that her grandparents were aware of the total collapse in her universe, they didn't talk about it. No one talked about it. Not her mom. Not her older brother. No one. And she was glad for that. She didn't want to talk about the pain of being left. And she had enough of her own pain without thinking about and feeling theirs too. She couldn't take on their pain with hers. She didn't want any of it. And she didn't want to have to hear those words hit the air.

But then there was Makenzie, and she was poking about with questions.

"Hey, where's your dad been? I haven't seen him for a while?" Makenzie asked while doing nothing but closely looking at Faith, and Faith knew that someone had to have told her.

"He's around . . ." And it wasn't a lie, he was around somewhere, she just didn't know where. At all.

"Oh yeah. Did he come and visit you in the Hospital much?" Faith thought about how bad of an investigator Makenzie would have been and challenged her with her response,

"Why?" Faith stared at Makenzie as if to say don't start, for her to just stop talking right then.

"Well I didn't see him at all when I was there, that's all." And Makenzie was ready to let the conversation die.

"You weren't there every day." Faith was defensive and tired. She didn't know what fight she was trying to win anymore. Now she was defending and protecting her dad.

"So he did come and visit you then. Okay." Makenzie stated it like a fact that she knew was a lie. As if it were a fine-you-win-I'm-done end of the conversation.

And Faith decided to let the truth go, "No."

"Why not . . . Fay . . ." Makenzie asked, but she had to have known.

The way Makenzie looked at her now made it feel like everybody knew.

"Mazie . . ." Faith pleaded with her voice not to crack, not to make this any harder to say than it already was, "he left . . . a few months ago . . ."

"What do you mean left? Like . . ."

The confusion on Makenzie's face told Faith that maybe she really didn't already know, she had probably just heard someone in the family talking about Faith's dad. From her response Faith could tell that this wasn't a scenario that Makenzie would have guessed.

"Yeah. Just. Left." Faith softly added.

And Faith noticed how Makenzie's eyes looked different, they were full of sadness, "Oh my God, Fay, . . ." Makenzie had the same exact worried and disgusted look on her face as when Faith had told her that Baskin Robbins had made a Ketchup flavored ice cream. "…Why didn't you tell me sooner?"

"Because," Faith shrugged her eyebrows, ". . . Every day. . . I thought he'd come back."

"Why would he do that . . . ?" Makenzie asked a question that was on a constant loop in Faith's mind and she didn't have an answer. The only answer Faith knew now was why he didn't come back.

{She wasn't enough.}

Makenzie

Makenzie took off the day's makeup standing in front of her Grandma's white antique dresser mirror while Faith shuffled in her overnight bag to pull out her Sunday church clothes for the next day. The pale blue painted walls of the room that hosted all of Makenzie and Faith's sleepovers were calming. Out of the three daughters their Grandmother had, their mothers were the oldest, and shared the exact same room growing up. But to Makenzie and Faith it would always be "their room."

Faith's bag rustled and Makenzie could hear the clanking of a hundred pills shaking back and forth in tall medicine containers. "Did you take your nighttime pills yet, Fay?" Makenzie asked reminding Faith, as if it was her disease too, and Makenzie started to take out her contacts for the night.

"No . . ." Faith sighed, "Ugh. I hate taking them, there's so many . . ." Makenzie knew that Faith already had to take 24 pills a day, not including the vitamin, iron, or folic acid pills, but she needed her to take them.

"Faithers, one day you will be shitting rainbows and butterflies, just little farts of joy, I promise you. It will be one great day, and I'll be there just dancing around the rainbows and butterflies too because I will just be so happy for you!" Makenzie made a little flutter around the room like a butterfly with her contact in one hand and came back to the center of the dresser. "But until then, you have to take that medicine. . . . Here, use my water . . ." Makenzie half-blind set her contact in its holder and lifted her tall water glass from the dresser with her other hand and held it over to Faith's side of the room. Faith sighed, walked over, and lifted the glass from her hand.

"Thanks . . ." Faith said annoyed, and Makenzie knew not to take it personally, that it was the pills and the disease that Faith was annoyed at, not her. She knew that before the disease, Faith hated even taking a Flintstone vitamin every day.

"You know . . . I don't know what I'd do without my dad, Fay. I just . . . don't." Makenzie had been thinking about it ever since Faith had told her about her dad. She had worried about losing her dad in so many ways and couldn't imagine what she would do if it happened for good.

"Mazie, we don't have to talk about this . . . I'm fine right now." Faith threw a handful of eight pills back against her open throat and took another gulp of water.

"I know, I'm just saying, I'm not fine with it. I'm not fine with your dad just leaving. I could seriously puke up a better parent than him, Fay. You don't deserve that. And I don't know what I would do if anything happened to my dad, it scares me to think about it . . ."

"But you and your dad fight all the time," Faith said, as if it would make losing him any easier.

"Yeah but, He's. My. Dad." Makenzie shook her head at Faith, "I'll never not love him."

"You don't hate your dad sometimes?" Faith asked, climbing into her twin bed and looking at Makenzie with squinting eyes.

"I mean I say that when I'm mad at him, but I don't think I could ever really hate him . . . why? Do you hate your dad now?" Makenzie flicked off the light at the doorway and walked over to her twin bed next to Faith's. The only light illuminating the room was the moon shining through sheer window curtains and the bright red numbers from the alarm clock set for 8 am.

"I dunno . . ." Faith said and looked like she was trying to picture something in the future as though Makenzie had just asked her what she'll be when she grew up. "Hey, what time is it?" Faith couldn't make out the red lines of the alarm clock from across the room.

"Ten forty-five . . ." Makenzie looked at the clock and then back at Faith all tucked in. Makenzie fixed her pillow behind her head and sank into it.

"We're too close to 11:11 now, we'd better stay up." Faith sighed.

"You're right, it will probably take us that long to decide what to wish for anyways." Makenzie laughed and fluffed her pillow.

"Not me. I already have mine." Faith said and rolled over, to look in the direction of the clock, waiting for a wish.

Death will paint everything a different shade of remorse.

You'll feel guilty that you're still breathing.
        But you can't stop.
You'll feel guilty for wanting to laugh again.
        And it will be awful the first time that you do.
You'll feel guilty for just about everything at first.
And someday, at some point, you'll start to feel guilty . . .
        for forgetting to feel guilty.

But of all Heaven's lessons, guilt isn't one of them. You don't need to hold on to it. It doesn't need to be a practice and it shouldn't be your life.

        Heaven would never approve of your guilt.
        Because Heaven has no regrets.

. . . .

My eyes adjust to new surroundings. I'm inside the house now. I'm aching and I can't stop feeling lost even though this place is so familiar.

I know exactly where I am, but I don't remember coming inside. I wonder if someone coaxed me in like a feral kitten hoping I would eat, or if they took me by the hand to drag me in. They could have probably just picked me up and carried me without trouble.

I've never felt so moveable in my life.

The house that isn't mine is filled with friends, and the house itself has this kind of embrace. This house has held more joy and more sadness than any house I've ever known, and its walls are seasoned in a way that makes every breath I take hurt a little less, because I can feel that this house understands. The door of this house has never been locked. The air in this house has never judged a soul. The furniture in this house has always consoled.

This house, and the people in it, are holding me together.

That's why I'm here.

But I can't stop asking myself why anyone, any of us, are really here. Why do we live if it's just to die? Why do we love if it's just to be left? Questions kink themselves inside my head and now I can't think about anything past them. I grab the couch beneath me and pull loose blankets and gather the fabric into my fist.

Someone inside the house, sitting across from me in the living room, is talking about her now and it hurts. It hurts so much just to hear them say her name but then they say something that hurts even more. They are using words like "was" and "had" to follow her name as she's talked about fondly, but those smallest words hold the opposite feeling. The first time someone talked about her in the past tense happened almost immediately, and it was too much yesterday and it's still too much today.

Those words hurt my ears just as much as it did hearing that she was gone for the first time. These stupid little meaningless and inactive verbs now hold a weight that pulls her further away from me. They will jump into every sentence and they will scream the loudest, forcing her into the past.

How can three letters bring me any more pain and how can I even prepare for more. I can't.

So I wait for someone else in the room to say the few words that never mattered to me before like "is" and "has" to describe her, just to bring her as close to the present as she can be. And as I've already noticed, many of the conversations eventually end, since all of this happened yesterday, with someone sighing and closing the conversation: "She is at peace now. She is happy."

I listen for these words and only when I hear that "she is," does breathing get a little easier. But nothing about this first full day without her is easy.

Everything, even things that didn't have her attached to them before, now have to be experienced without her and it's like starting all over again. Even things that I could physically do without her before simply cannot be done as easily.

Just knowing that she isn't here, makes the act of doing them impossible.

Like sleeping.

I'm so tired right now but I don't know how I'll ever sleep again. The first day without her should have bled me dry of life and it should have fed me a depression that kept me sleeping for the rest of time.

But it didn't.

It did the opposite.

It gave me too much pain to sleep.

And I couldn't allow myself to stop refusing the night, and to stop fighting every second without her.

I tried to sleep last night. I did. But not for me. For everyone else. The girl with the dimples brushed my back with her fingertips like a mother soothing a child to sleep and she pet my hair until my sniffles softened. She was there for me. To watch me. To make sure I was okay. *"I've got her,"* the girl with the dimples lovingly told everyone else in the living room of the house as they fought sleep, volunteering that she would take the midnight watch. Without saying the words of it, I knew that the current situation had automatically placed me on suicide watch.

But I would fall into sleep for only a moment before jolting awake. Like there was a lightning bolt of memories re-surfacing and I needed to wake up and remember them all one by one, before they were gone too.

And I'd try to close my eyes again but my body would shake from the absence of crying. My body resuscitating itself in an attempt to manually keep my heart pumping. To keep me here.

I'd try again and again to close my eyes through the night but after only sleeping for a moment my lungs would refill gasping for air, quickly and loudly, catching my breath from the pain of the heartache and hours of heavy sobbing.

But more than my body keeping me from sleep was a single fear. One thought that I couldn't stand. . . . The thought of waking up to this. To waking up and losing her all over again to a new day. I couldn't bear the thought of going through it again.

I couldn't risk the first moments climbing awake from dreams without her. I couldn't set myself up for the pain of having to remind myself that she was gone.

Even worse, I was afraid of it being carved so deep in my soul that I would wake up just knowing.

I've never lost the same person so many times, and I've never been so afraid of losing them again, even after they were already gone.

Faith

She didn't want to talk about how her dad left. Beyond the fact that she didn't want to admit it, or that there was really nothing to talk about, she hated how people would always react. And she didn't want to give people, anyone at all, strangers or not, the opportunity. Because they would always respond by asking two questions. First they'd ask, *"Why would he leave you?"* maybe with a gasp or an appalled face to show empathy. Maybe they'd show disgust.

Even worse, they might look sorry for her.

That was the worst.

They'd ask why he would leave her as if it were a new question and hadn't been already burning in Faith's guts for months. That question ate at her sanity. That question ripped her insides into tiny bloody pieces. And she hated hearing it out loud. Giving the feeling of abandonment words, was like giving it legs. Saying it out loud was like her dad walking out again and again.

But the second question, after Faith would feel the pain of wondering, "What was wrong with her," they would ask what was wrong with him as in, *"What kind of person does that?"* But she had no answers. She didn't know. And the emptiness drove further into her gut and cut up her insides in a way so painful, that she would never be able to find the words to tell people. All she could give them was the silent look with a shrug and quizzical eyes that said *"I guess leaving me is worth feeling like a shame-filled coward the rest of someone's life."*

She hated to think that he may have actually weighed the pros and cons of leaving. That it was worth it to him to spend his life in hiding, like a criminal. That running away from her was worth it. Like she was some kind of jail sentence that he just couldn't be stuck in anymore.

To him, freedom was greater than love.

She hated that.

Because she had always thought that love was freedom.

But she was wrong.

She was wrong about everything.

Makenzie

She went into the bathroom and she didn't want to, but she did it.
She couldn't explain why. But she just had to do it.
Because until she did it, there would be something clawing at her
stomach and her throat. There would be a constant knocking on her brain of
feelings and words that would just repeat over and over again replaying
triggers until she succumbed to defeat.

She locked the door behind her with a push of her pointer finger into
the center of the door handle, and sighed just under her breath.
She was alone.
She was in control.

She didn't look in the mirror as she walked by the bathroom sink,
because she already knew what she looked like. She looked like a girl with a
lot of problems and she didn't need to look into those familiar disappointed
pain-filled eyes.

Makenzie's eyes were leading a double life, they would look sparkly
and happy in photographs with friends but when she was alone she hated
those eyes. They knew everything. And they reminded her of what she tried
so hard to forget.
She didn't want to think about what those eyes would say right now.

Not now.
Not with what she was about to do.
She clenched her jaw, in her head inventorying everything inside of
her that she needed to get rid of.
She unclenched her jaw, and filled her lungs with all the shame of
how much she had just eaten.

Makenzie bent down on to her knees and while pulling her hair back
with the hair tie from her wrist she wished things could be different. She
wished things could be easier. She wished she didn't feel the way she felt.
She just wanted to feel better.
Instead she felt nauseated about everything.

Makenzie took two fingers from her right hand and pulled them close to her face. She let herself admit to feelings of guilt, anxiousness, and regret to deepen the wave of nausea in her stomach. She let herself feel every ounce of disappointment and sadness that she had been deflecting, as she looked into the toilet water reflecting back at her. The outline of her face reflecting in the bowl of water made her envision that she was indeed exactly what she already felt like—a pile of shit. The base of the toilet bowl looked like an underwater cave, undiscovered, and she stared at the opening through the clear water. The opening that will make everything disappear. She stared at it and tried to keep her eyes open and focused on it as long as she could.

She took a deep breath and because the very tips of her fingers already smelled of the warm tar of cigarettes, they aided in the intense need to help her vomit as she forced them into the back of her mouth. She thought about the smell of the toilet water. She breathed in that smell through her mouth. She thought about how the vessel that was perched in front of her held such foul secrets.

Her fingers touched the back of her tongue.

And as her insides reacted, she braced herself.

She had done it enough times before to know how to purge without making a sound. It was one of the things she was good at. One of the only things she could control. Water, undigested food, and acid came up, making small splashes inside the toilet bowl. Chewed macaroni still mostly whole, swirled around slowly in a liquid that looked like Thousand Island dressing. The contents of Makenzie's stomach mixed with the water already in the toilet, made it expand and look as though she had gotten rid of three times as much from inside her as what she actually did.

The amount of disgust in the toilet made her feel accomplished. It made her feel less disgusting herself. She was no longer carrying all of that around in her. She felt lighter.

And when she felt like she had gotten it all out—the sadness, the anger, the lack of control—then it was done. But it was never over.

She pulled at the roll of toilet paper and blew her nose. Shards of food, however tiny they may be, burned deep in her nose cavities. She folded the tissue in half and in half again and threw it in the toilet with the rest of herself. The tissue stuck to the surface, like a small paper boat floating in a lake of devastation.

She pushed down the handle on the toilet as she stood up and timed a little cough to clear her throat as the toilet flushed. She made sure that all of the evidence went down with the flush and that it wouldn't need another.

Her eyes instinctively began to water; she had tried hard to keep them open wide and looking up while she puked, but they were still leaking. So she pulled just one square of toilet paper off the roll and wrapped the white tissue around her pointer finger. She looked into the mirror but ignored her reflection. She swiped upward at her mascaraed eyelashes with her homemade toilet paper wand to steal the wetness from them to keep her mascara from smudging.

To keep people from knowing.

She pulled her hair tie out of her hair and returned it to her wrist. She raised her eyebrows in the mirror as she questioned if she looked like someone who had just thrown up. And when her face became less flushed, her eyes stopped watering, and the answer to that questions was "no," Makenzie would return to the real world. She pulled her jeans straight at the bend where they had bunched from kneeling, and she ran her hands around the bottom of her shirt while tugging it.

She opened the bathroom door with a turn and the lock popped back out like the signal at the end of a timer.

It was done.

And she would convince herself that she felt better, but she never did.

{About anything.}

Faith

Makenzie made a dash to the beauty aisle as they entered the Rite Aid two blocks up from their Grandma's house. Faith meandered behind. The first winter without her dad made December feel like its own disease.

"oO! What do you think about this color!" Makenzie bent over and held up a green nail polish bottle that was so electrifying the sun would have taken a break.

"Eh," Faith knew Makenzie wouldn't actually have gotten that one. Makenzie liked to match her outfits too much to pick a color that only matched the 90s.

"What about this . . . ?" Makenzie reached for a peacock blue—raising her eyebrows waiting for Faith's response. ". . . C'mon your favorite!"

"It's too bright." Faith shrugged it off knowing well that Makenzie would have bought the blue nail polish just for her even though the only thing Makenzie owned that was blue were blue jeans. "Get whatever you want. I don't feel like painting my nails tonight." Faith didn't feel like doing anything.

"I'll paint your nails for you, Faithers!" Makenzie stood up and nudged Faith a smile.

Faith didn't feel like smiling.

Christmas music was blaring through the store's speakers. "Ugh what is this song . . .?" Faith winced at the lyrics *"Happy holiday happy holiday, happy holiday while the merry bells keep ringing may your every wish come true."*

"Happy Holiday!" Makenzie sarcastically widened her eyes and Faith pressed her lips together hoping that Makenzie wouldn't break out in song and dance in the middle of the store.

As Makenzie just darted off to the feminine care aisle, Faith whispered, "Oh do you need tampons . . . ?" She fell back behind Makenzie and waited at the end of the aisle.

Makenzie looked all around before grabbing the biggest pack of adult diapers she could find. And Makenzie started to dance with the 46 pack of large pads. In a baritone voice she mimicked the song and sang "Happy holiday" as if she were waltzing with 46 diapers all at once.

"Mazie . . . stop." Faith shook her head and walked in from the end of the aisle.

Makenzie just continued singing, "Happy holiday," and as Faith got closer Makenzie lofted the pack in the air so high that it cleared the aisle height and everyone in the store could see there was some extra activity going on in the world of feminine care.

"Makenzie!" Faith whispered loudly.

The pack came down with a *splat* on the ground and Faith looked at Makenzie with reprimanding eyes.

"You should have caught it." Makenzie looked at Faith disappointedly.

Makenzie bent over to pick up the large pack of plastic diaper pads and Faith felt relieved. She didn't want to play Makenzie's silly game. But instead of putting the pack back, Makenzie picked up another one and was now holding two large diaper bundles, one in each arm.

Faith shook her head and started to back away.

"Hey, Faith!" Makenzie talked over the song and sang, "Happy holiday," looking like she was going to juggle the over-sized packs but instead she launched one right at Faiths head.

Faith caught it with a loud plastic *smack* and as soon as she realized that she was holding it—she lofted it back to Makenzie.

And as if Makenzie knew that Faith would throw it right back, Makenzie released the other pack towards her with the same timing.

Faith caught it, pissed at the rhythm and timing Makenzie had.

She lofted the second pack back at Makenzie. Trying to discard it faster than the last, but Makenzie kept up with her speed releasing another one in Faith's direction.

Faith caught it and threw it back quicker than the last.

And finally realizing that this was probably the first game ever held of "Hot-Potato" with jumbo adult diaper packs, Faith let out a giggle. And once a giggle came out, she felt like laughing.

The sound of hands smacking plastic echoed through the store.

Makenzie could always make her laugh.

Even when it was the last thing Faith wanted to do.

Makenzie

It was the first snowfall of the year. The one that always felt the most magical, like each and every snowflake falling down was something you could catch in your palm and make a wish on.

Faith and Makenzie flung their Grandmother's screen door open like children half their age, wearing gloves and scarves racing out to catch falling snowflakes. They were closer in age to adults than children, and because of that Makenzie ran right out into the middle of the street to play and twirl around in the untouched snow.

Makenzie bent her neck back and squinted her eyes at the wet mists of snowflakes hitting her eyelashes. She stared up at the sky and could see each snowflake big and round fall faster down to her. Her strawberry blonde hair was already collecting snowflakes, sprinkled on top of her making her sparkle. She couldn't see anything but snowflakes, coming down one by one, first fast and then they seemed to move in slow motion as they got closer to her, as she could see each one separately. She held her glove-covered hands outward and up towards the sky and closed her eyes. She felt a peace and a calmness that only the first snow can bring. And she heard a *chick* and a giggle.

She looked over and saw Faith had pulled her phone out of her pocket and taken a picture; Makenzie smiled and reached for the camera, and Faith surrendered it.

Makenzie took hold of Faith's phone and pointed the camera lens end at Faith posing stoically in her matching blue hat and glove set. Just over and past Faith's shoulder was a stop sign that had snow clinging to its face. With Faith centered in the snow and the stop sign behind her, Makenzie took a picture.

Makenzie gave the phone back to Faith and looked around on the ground for a perfect spot of untouched snow. One that didn't have their shoe prints frolicking in it yet. She found a spot and bent over reaching to wipe her finger up and down through the snow. Her gloved pointer finger stretched out as far as it could to carve letters into the fresh canvas. She backed up and revealed her masterpiece while shaking the wetness from her gloves.

"Take a pic, Fay!" Makenzie had written it for her.

The letters in the snow read:
"Mazie & Fay" with the date.
"This is going to be our year!" Makenzie announced out loud like she had just claimed the middle of the street. The snow celebrated the season and Makenzie knew they were going to get through anything together.

Faith smiled and nodded her head. The camera app on her phone made another *chick* as Faith took the picture.

Comfort is gone.
But it's not dead.

You may not realize it right now, but everyone you know will be trying to comfort you, to build you back up. They will all try so hard to help you to sigh, to smile, to laugh again.

They will toss gestures your way like cushions into the bottom of the endless pit that you're falling into. And only once you hit the bottom . . . days, months, maybe years from now, will you find the comfort that they were trying to give to you then. You'll finally see it all once you're able to feel again. And you will eventually, one day, find the words to thank them.

· · · · · · · ·

I pull my legs up beside me and put my dirty bare feet on the couch. Now that the sun has risen and the clocks are still moving, there's nothing I can do. I stare at the clocks in the living room and wish that they would have stopped yesterday. I wished that they could just be blinking blank eights across all the digital panels. Flashing the feeling of a short circuit. I wish that time really could have just ended with her, instead of just feeling like it did. I don't trust the clocks. I don't believe them. I don't believe anything anymore.

I watch the teal colors of the digital clock in front of the tv go from 2:21 to 2:22. But there isn't anything to wish for anymore. There's nothing left. So I close my eyes and squeeze them tight as if I were making a wish, and in my head, I tell her that I love her. My only wish is that she will hear it. That maybe there are angels that catch wishes floating up and deliver messages like answered prayers. And maybe, somehow, she can find a way to whisper back that she loves me too.

I'll wait for it, but I already know.

I hear the door open to the house that isn't mine, like I've heard it open and close so many times in the last 24 hours. But this time there is someone new standing there. I squint, and I force my stinging eyes to focus, but all that I see is blue fuzz. Right away, the blue fuzzy shape reminds me of her.

Behind a giant blue fuzzy stuffed animal is the girl with the tattoos. She's holding it tightly and I can see her face poking out from behind it. She's standing in the doorway. And she's broken. Her face is paler than I ever thought it could be, and her eyes are red. She holds her eyes open wide and holds out the blue stuffed animal in front of her, towards me. She looks like she just won a carnival prize in hell.

"This . . . is for you. I wanted to bring you something. I didn't know what, but then I thought of this Lilo and Stitch doll. I know how much you guys loved that movie. And no matter what it cost I wanted to get you the biggest one they had . . ." I reach out and take it and the girl with the tattoos looks even emptier without the stuffed animal in her hands now.

I hug her the best I can while still sitting and crying and repeat my cousin and my favorite quote from that Hawaiian Disney movie, "Ohana . . . means family, and family means . . . nobody gets left behind . . . or forgotten." Tears come out of me faster as I realize that the quote has a whole new meaning now. I squeeze the stuffed animal and I acknowledge to myself that I was afraid of forgetting about her. I was afraid of time taking more and more of her away from me.

But now, at least for now, I have this reminder that it can't. Time can't ever take her from me again. And I think about the girl with the tattoos and how this is the nicest thing that anyone has ever done for me. Maybe people did nicer things for me before. I can't remember them. I can only feel this new life that is only a day old and filled with so much pain.

The girl with the tattoos sits down on the couch and into the same pain. She knows that this new life won't be easy. She knows. And in this new life where everyone is constantly asking me if I need anything and begging me to tell them what can they do, she didn't waste a lung's worth of air asking such rhetorical and generic things. She thought about what she could do. And she brought me a memory and a piece of hope.

I squeeze the big blue stuffed animal tight into my chest against my sore heart, hoping it can help to slow the sobs that are still trying to catch up to yesterday's tears. I am balled up on the couch and close my eyes, trying to just stop the tears, but they don't stop. There's no stopping them. The buildup of salt on my contacts burns and stings sharp like sand and shampoo being in my eyes at the same time. Closing them burns even more, but I welcome the pain.

With my eyes glued shut, I feel someone lay a blanket over me and it doesn't feel bad, but I can't reach the words to thank them. I still can't stop wishing that each and every person in this room were her. Yet at the exact same time I hope that the ones here never leave. I feel the heaviness of only living in a contradiction and only wanting impossible things.

I hear someone else come over. They step right into my sorrow and they lift my head up gently from the couch, lowering it back into their lap.

My head is pounding from all of the tears I've cried and it's even heavier from the ones I've held back. They start to trickle fingers over my hair and I can feel that it's the girl with the dimples. She doesn't care that my hair is knotted and filled with days of dirt and snot. Her fingers just want to soothe me. I try to travel to the place in my mind that her gentle loving sweeping wants to take me. I work hard to imagine peace. I imagine that her fingers are angel wings brushing past my face. I think of soft blues and greens and clouds whisking gently like the fingertips petting my hair.

My eyes are closed, but they feel open.
I can see everything now. . .
I can picture her, finally. . .
She's in a vast openness of nothing but calm air and swirls of colors. She's quiet, but smiling. And she's waving at me in a T-shirt and jeans. Her joy is calming. She's so excited that even the air around her is smiling. I can feel the energy of her having a thousand things to tell me.
Her eyes are bright with stories.
I can't wait to hear them all.
I wait for her to say something, anything. But she's just smiling. And I want to hug her so bad, but we're separated by too much air. The air around me is too dark and heavy. It's not the same air she's in. It's different. The air around me is getting foggy and gray. My heart starts to break as she's standing in the same place but she's moving further and further from me now. And I'm moving further from her. And before I lose her again, I tell her something that I know she already knows,
"I love you!" I shout in my mind across the air. She's still there, standing, smiling, and I wait for her to say it back to me.
But she doesn't.
She says something else instead.
She tells me something I already know.
Excitedly, she lifts two words over the fog into my air. Two words that come to me gentle but loud. She sends the words through the air to me and they're coming into my whole body so that I can feel every syllable of them. They are short, but strong. And her smile is encouraging.

She's getting further and further from me now, but her eyes say that she won't ever be too far. . .

But just like that she's gone.

Again.

The fog sets in all around me.

And I'm back to seeing only gray.

It's always gray anymore.

I can feel tears collecting down the side of my face that I'm lying on, my sobs heavy as my eyes are still closed and everything feels so closed now. The girl with the dimples keeps petting my hair, with two hands now, trying to fan the flames of my cries before they get too out of control. But I can't do anything to stop them. I can only lift my head and try to tell her what just happened. I wipe tears from my mouth to try to move sniffles away for sounds to come out.

I've got to tell her the message.

Heaven's message is Earth's experience.

Through sobs, I sit up and I repeat the two words to the girl with the dimples. She nods her head with leaking eyes. I echo them again, to the others sitting around the room. I wish I could tell them more, but I'm just shaking my head. And they are all nodding theirs now, all of their heads looking heavy from the weight of tears behind eyes.

I pull the words back from the air and I wrap them around me. And finally now, holding the stuffed animal tight to my chest and holding on to those two little words in my mind, I let out a sigh.

I believe her.

I always believed her.

I take another deep breath, trying to calm my shuddering body. And I remind myself that for the rest of my life, I will remember her smile and her telling me,

"No Regrets."

Makenzie

"Fay, this is it!" Makenzie ran her fingers along the body of a black Jetta, the car she had wanted since forever. The car in front of her was freshly washed and shiny reflecting sunbeams like a black diamond.

"Yeah, that's nice." Faith barely looked at the car before walking past to the other used cars in the small lot.

"I just can't believe they have my exact car here! Too bad it won't still be here by the time I can drive next year . . ." Makenzie cupped both her hands around her eyes to create a viewing shield against the driver's window to see into the dark car and soak up every detail of her dream car. She pictured how she would look inside the car and how great it would look without all the cheap tags of information taped to it. After she was done looking into the car, Makenzie stretched her hands out alongside it as far as they could go and pressed her cheek into the driver's window and gave the car a big hug. Her cheek quickly tingled warm like sunburn from the black of the car sucking in the sun's heat.

"Oh look at this one!" Faith pointed to a shitty little beat-up red four door.

"Eh, it's alright." Makenzie wasn't going to waver, she was loyal to her Jetta.

"You like red!? Besides, I'm not going to get your exact dream car for my first car." Faith kept walking further and further away from the black Jetta, looking at each and every car.

"Well what's your dream car, anyways?" Makenzie started to follow her and could see small drops of rain polka dot the black top before feeling a drop herself.

"I dunno, any car that drives." Faith sounded desperate.

"So you don't care what color or style it is? What if your first car is some ratty old station wagon?" Makenzie jumped in front of an old wagon-looking car and held a cheesy grin on her face with her arms outstretched like that car was a game show prize.

"Okay, so a station wagon wouldn't be my first pick." Faith shook her head at Makenzie and laughed.

"Oh well, we should head back, it's starting to rain." Makenzie looked up at the sky and headed back to the side of the lot that her Jetta was on, closest to Faith's house. Faith followed.

"So you think you'll come down here and buy a car soon?" Makenzie asked as they climbed the sidewalk on the hill. She bent over in mid-stride and reached for a dandelion weed that was growing in the small section of uncut grass between the sidewalk and the curb. Makenzie pulled out the once golden weed that was now faded and stared at it for only a second before blowing on it hard like it was a cake with one hundred little white fluffy candles that she needed to extinguish in one breath in order to make her wish come true.

"I dunno, prolly not. They seemed expensive here." Faith looked back at the lot over her shoulder down the hill and bent down to pick up a weed for a wish too.

"Yeah, a little bit." Makenzie started to walk more briskly, wanting to run from the rain, "C'mon, let's run the rest of the way, it's only a block."

"It's not that far." Faith held her walking speed and Makenzie was getting hit with more large drops of rain.

"C'mon, I'm getting all wet, dude." Makenzie started to jog but was turned back waiting for Faith to join her. And Faith sat down on the sidewalk. "What are you doing? C'mon!" Makenzie could hear the rain hitting the roofs of the houses along the street beside her.

"Just come here a second, then I'll run with you." Faith sounded exhausted and fanned her hand into her chest motioning Makenzie to come to her, the other hand still holding a wish.

"What the heck, Fay, are you feeling okay, what's wrong?" Makenzie sat down on the edge of the curb with her knees bent up to her chest. She was tense, ready to carry Faith home on her back if she had to.

"Just . . . sit for a minute. It's not going to kill you. It's just rain." Faith sat on the curb with her back straight, her eyes closed and her head tilted back to the sky. Faith smiled a little smirk.

"You feel okay though?" Makenzie still wondered if Faith was having one of her stomach attacks or if her heart was hurting her.

"Yeah, I just like to feel things. Ya know? The rain, it feels good sometimes, you don't always have to run from it. It doesn't have to be a bad feeling, it can feel good if you just let it wash over you. Don't always be in such a rush. Just feel it for a minute and once you feel it, we can go." Faith took a deep breath and sighed.

"Okay . . ." Makenzie sat and tried to relax but her butt was hurting from the cement edge and she was starting to feel cold from the rain already. The rain didn't feel good to Makenzie at all, instead it sent a chill up her spine and it made her worry that if Faith thought it felt good that she might be feverish again from all of the inflammation in her body. She knew Faith wouldn't complain about it, but before she could ask her how she was feeling again, Faith interrupted her.

"Are you feeling it?" Faith asked.

"Yeah . . ."

"Alright, now we can go . . ." Faith stood up and smiled. She blew on the dandelion wish still in her hand, making all of the little white puffs of seeds fly to the ground before ditching the stem into the raindrop-stained-street. And she started to jog. Her eyes widened at Makenzie as if to say "race you home."

Faith

It was advertised as a black Buick Century with a line underneath it that said "great first car." That car ought to be aged to perfection, it was almost as old as Faith was herself. Faith had been scanning the Sunday Classifieds Auto section for weeks trying to figure out the difference in costs from a car that "runs fairly good" to one that was in "fair condition." The overuse of the word "fair" in most of the lower priced ads made the offer seem anything but, especially the ones sold "as is."

But this ad, this one literally jumped out and told her this would be a good first car. It might be beat up, but it would run. And as long as the car ran, then she would be able to run whenever she needed to.

The cost of the car was exactly the amount that Faith had saved from her first few months working her after school job. It was a perfect. Faith excitedly showed Makenzie the classified ad that had a big fresh ink circle around it and the girls' eyes widened at the same time.

Faith folded up the paper excitedly and made sure the big circle part was on top. Makenzie folded up the comic section of the newspaper, stood up, and went back to the room to pack her things.

But by the time Faith met Makenzie in their room at their Grandma's house, she was deflated. "My mom said we can't get it because we can't afford it." Faith tossed the paper on to the bed while she pulled out the top left drawer of the antique white dresser that held Faith's money she was saving and she started to count it as if her mom were lying.

"But you have the exact amount and it's your money, what does she mean you can't get it?!" Makenzie already had her shoes on. Faith knew that Makenzie didn't understand the way things went. They didn't have any money since her dad left. They barely could afford food, and any extra money they had went to paying past due bills so that the heat and electric wouldn't get turned off. Faith's mom couldn't help her with tags, titles, inspection, car insurance, or gas money. And Faith knew not to push the subject because the only place pushing it would take the conversation would be for Faith's mom to say out loud that she was sorry but that Faith's dad left her with all the bills. Everything always came back to Faith's dad leaving.

Everything was still a rippling disappointment from his one choice.

"Because there's titles, and tags, and plate fees, and apparently it costs money to do everything you need to in order to make a car officially yours, not to mention the gas to put in it." Faith sighed thinking if she would have bought the car she would have had to push it home until she got her next paycheck.

"Oh. Well how much is all that. It can't be that much. It can't be like more than the car itself." Makenzie tried to lighten the situation to make it seem not that far out of reach.

"I dunno, money I don't have. Maybe next week it will still be there and . . ."

"Fay, how much is all that stuff the fees, how much extra?" Makenzie didn't get that it didn't matter.

"I don't know like a couple hundred, I dunno . . ." Faith was done counting the money she had; it was still only the same amount it was ten minutes ago and she folded it neatly into a stack and put it back in the top left drawer. Faith started to slide the heavy antique drawer shut.

"Fay, wait . . ." Makenzie reached for her bag and pulled out her wallet. Makenzie lifted the folded white piece of paper from the longer section in the back of her wallet and reached towards Faith.

Faith didn't know what Makenzie was doing but started shaking her head.

"Here." Makenzie firmly held out the check in her hand, with an insistent tone with underplayed excitement. "It's my check, I just got paid this week and I didn't even cash it yet." It took her two weeks of work to earn it, but in a second she gave it all away.

"Mazie, I'm not taking your money! That's your very first check from your first job, you need that for other things, I'll get a car soon either way. I'm not taking your money." Faith closed the drawer.

"Exactly. This is my first check from my first job, and so I don't even know what it's like to have money yet." Makenzie laughed, "I was just saving it to buy something good!"

"I'm not taking your money, Mazie!"

"Fay. Listen to me. We are doing this. You are taking my check. And we are getting that car. Today. No regrets."

There was no arguing now. Faith knew that saying "no regrets" was the end of the conversation. It was the most serious thing they could ever say to each other, more serious than swearing on baby Jesus and more permanent than a middle-finger-swear.

Makenzie smirked as her hand pushed the check on to Faith. And Makenzie's feet bounced up and down against the side of the bed ready for an adventure.

Makenzie

Makenzie couldn't believe that they were actually on their way to look at the car, that it could actually be that easy. She wished they would have thought of it sooner. Christ, having a car could be the answer to so many problems. A set of wheels that turn so fast they might lift them right off the ground. She wished for wings to fly away, but soon enough the girls would have wheels and that was close enough.

Wheels would be just as good.

They didn't need to go far, they just needed to know that they weren't stuck. That if they needed to they could leave.

"Dude, 2:22!" Makenzie pointed through the space in between Faith's mom driving the van and Faith in the passenger seat. The numbers lined up perfectly behind the digital glass were a nudge to believe that everything else falling into place might not be too far behind. Makenzie's fingers were already crossed as soon as she saw the numbers in a row like a slot machine jackpot in bright teal dashes.

She closed her eyes and she made a wish.

Makenzie opened her eyes once her wish was done and saw Faith's fingers still crossed and her eyes still closed.

Faith's mom pulled up to a two-story Victorian house with blue shutters and a two-car garage. Makenzie saw the black car outside in the exact center of the driveway, unlike anyone would pull it in to park, more like it was on show.

"There it is, Fay!" Makenzie was the first to see it through the front windshield crouching over the hump of the back seat. Faith was silent but smiled, and Makenzie wondered how Faith could contain herself in a moment like this, how she was not hanging out the window like a dog right now. Makenzie was testing her own extreme will not to jump out of the car and high five the entire neighborhood that surrounded this car that they were looking at.

And there Faith was with just a quiet smile.

Makenzie jumped out of the back of her aunt's car and walked anxiously behind Faith, to look at the car on display in the driveway.

It was black, as promised. The back bumper of the car was faded and there were spots along the wheel well of the tire that had rust spreading. The car looked aged from years of sun, the hood and the trunk were slightly lighter in color than the sides of the car.

The tires were gray with wear.

The car was old.

It was used.

{It was a treasure.}

The car was well aged, but the raised circular emblem of the Buick logo shimmered in the sun as if to say it had plenty of adventures left in it.

Faith

"I love this song!" Faith claimed the song and beat Makenzie to turning up the dial in their new used car. Faith placed her hands back on the steering wheel and looked at Makenzie wide eyed with a look of accomplishment.

Makenzie sang the song so loud as if they girls were in the front row of a concert just then and the lead singer in the band were reaching out from the radio with a microphone right in front of Makenzie. Faith laughed and tried to sing just as loud.

And because the car was in park, sitting in front of Faith's house, their singing shook the whole car.

Faith leaned the driver's seat all the way back and raised her hands to the ceiling, stretching to take up and touch every ounce of vehicle space she could like she was the winning driver in a race car videogame.

Makenzie's feet were up on the dashboard and her toes wiggled as she painted her toenails one by one with a little black brush. Faith could see from her seat that they were becoming red and she smiled at Makenzie's ability to multitask without missing a single lyric.

The car felt less like a vehicle to get them to destinations than it felt like a destination itself. It held all of the excitement of an escape plan, and all of the comforts of home.

A new song came on the radio and Faith and Makenzie's eyes lit up.

Every song, as long as it had come out of the car's radio, was their song.

Makenzie

"Hey, Fay?" Makenzie looked up at Faith from a Star magazine she was holding, "do you ever want to go look for your dad sometime, you know, now that you can drive and have a car? I mean I'll go with you anywhere you want to go, just tell me when . . . we could take a weekend and stay somewhere." Makenzie tried to make it seem like a fun casual weekend escape to the beach and not a pointless adventure spent trying to find a needle in a haystack that had been missing for almost a year.

"Eh, doubt it. I have no idea where he is, he could be anywhere." Faith shrugged her shoulders, "besides, what do you say when you find someone who left you behind, 'gotcha'? I found you? Tag you're it?" Faith made a face at the situation and shrugged her shoulders again. Makenzie knew Faith couldn't just keep shrugging it off though, it had to hurt.

"So you're just going to give up and not look for him at all?" Makenzie couldn't imagine not wanting to at least yell at him or ask him for answers or find out if he was okay.

"Makenzie. I'm not the one giving up . . . I'm not the one who left." Makenzie could see the pain in Faith's face as her forehead tightened and her jaw clenched.

"Alright, I know . . . I just figured now that we had a car that you'd want to go. I just want to make sure that you won't regret not looking for him one day." Makenzie turned the next page in the magazine while still looking at Faith. "So, no regrets if you don't look for him?"

"Yup. No regrets." Faith made deep eye contact with Makenzie, "I'm not the one who left. It's not my mistake to regret."

And Makenzie realized that there really was nothing that Faith could regret.

It was his choice to be gone.

It was always his choice.

The Planning

When tragedy comes, all future plans are voided.
  In an instant.
  Except one.
  And the only "plan" that's left is the worst, most god-awful plan, ever.

What you'll want to do, more than anything,
  is to just lie in a bed,
    or a ditch,
      and wait for time to bury you.

  It will feel impossible to even think about doing anything of value, or anything as "planned" ever again.
  But you will have to.
  Because there is one itinerary that needs finalized—immediately.
  And the planning of it will be the most painful, most agonizing thing you've ever in your whole life had to do.

  But it is the planning of it that will keep you alive . . .
  Because it will keep you breathing.
    It will keep you thinking about the future.
    And it will keep you moving.

  Because you have a job to do.
    And you don't want to let Heaven down.

. . . .

I look around the room and I see the notebook that I had asked for earlier on the table with a pen. I don't remember when or how it got there but I let myself feel glad to see it. And only because there is something else for me to hold on to, do I then lessen my grip on the blue stuffed animal and place it beside me.

I flip to the first ruled page. And I start to write like I would start any other message to her . . .

"Hey Best Friend,"

. . . and then I don't know what to tell her first. I don't know how to start. It seems silly. But there is so much to tell her . . . and so I start by telling her what happened. I put my pen to the paper focusing on moving it, but it doesn't move.

I don't know if I can say it yet. As angry as I am I don't even think I can carve it out into the paper with this pen. I can't let the words come together to repeat what actually did happen. Not even the pen in my hand will betray my heart to let those words come together.

But that's okay, I don't need to say it. It would only hurt more to see it in ink. And then there's the unsure feeling that she might already know more about what happened to her since yesterday than I do, so instead, I start with telling her what happened to me . . .

"Yesterday, I died. And today, I think I died even more . . ."

My hand moves across three pages, filling them effortlessly with things that happened yesterday, without admitting the cause of all the events. Words pour out of me on to paper like tears and I feel lighter now. Now that I've written down all the things I needed to remember to tell her, all of the things that she's missed so far, my memory is under less pressure.

Three people sit in the first room inside the house, watching me. They are just watching. Just waiting.

For me to cry again, to hug me, waiting for their cue to play back the sequence of "it's okay," "I miss her too," and "she's in a better place now's."

They are all just paused.

So I stop writing and I look up.

They ask me what there is to do today, and what they can help me with. They want to know what all needs to be done before *that day*. Before the Funeral. And I wonder if it's too late to order a box for me too. Is there still time for me to go with her? I've wondered since the moment she left how I can leave too. And I know that they know that. But that isn't the planning that they're talking about.

And I shrug my shoulders and take a big slow breath.

I stare.

Unblinkingly.

At the air in the center of the room.

I take another deep breath.

And I try to mentally create the worst to-do list ever.

Makenzie

At the grocery store Faith flipped through the different kinds of packaged bologna meat in the cooled trough-like grocery store display bin and found a pack of thick-cut bacon. "I need bacon." Faith turned to Makenzie and the girl with the tattoos and asked, "do you guys want any bacon tonight?"

"Yeah, sure, I guess . . . ?" Makenzie tried not to let the expression on her face sour as she thought about bacon. She could see from the package that more than half of the strips of bacon were just thick white glistening sections. In the very center of each strip was a small outline of meat the color of ham hugged by thick creamy fat on all sides.

When Faith grabbed a second package of bacon Makenzie's eyes widened and her head shook fiercely. She looked to the girl with the tattoos for reassurance, "We don't need a whole 'nother pack, how much are you going to eat?"

"Well, I'm going to eat a whole pound myself, so if you want some too then we should get two pounds." Faith said it confidently, desperately, and almost surprised that she was even asking. "Listen, they wouldn't let me leave the Hospital until I gained weight and I'm supposed to be still gaining weight, every visit since they've been asking me why I'm not gaining weight and they look at me like they want to do more tests and stuff. And now I'm losing weight again! I just can't. I can't let them know that I'm not holding on weight or they're going to give me even more steroids and what if they make me stay in the Hospital again!? I need to be at least one hundred pounds again. My next appointment's next week!" Faith was frantic over a pound.

Makenzie could sympathize.

"Here," Makenzie held out her hand to Faith but Makenzie's hand was empty, "get the two packs, I'll make them for you and you can eat as much as you want." Makenzie bounced her empty open hand in the air, and Faith looked like a little kid that was just allowed to get two toys in the store instead of one. She handed Makenzie the two pounds of bacon and smiled wide.

"Thanks, Mazie, you're the best!"

Thinking of the two pounds of pure fat Makenzie held in her hands made her feel nervous, but it was for Faith.

She'd do anything for her.

Faith

She thought that monthly checkups were for babies and that remission was only for people with cancer. She was neither, but today she had both.

The Nurse that weighed her in had a generic patterned scrub with teal, yellow, and pink swirls. Shapes of nothingness. She held Faith's chart while asking "Date of birth?"

Faith mumbled her birthday and the Nurse followed along on her chart; only after Faith confirmed her birthdate did the Nurse then call her by her name.

"Alright, Faith, I need you to sit down here and I'll take your blood pressure and your temperature and then we'll weigh you in."

Faith sat silently staring at the large scale behind the Nurse as she gave the Nurse her left arm; within seconds her bicep was being wrapped and suffocated. With every hand pump of the Nurse's palm on the end of the rubber hose Faith's left arm went from tight, to tingly, to numb. She wiggled her fingers and couldn't feel them. The armband tightened and tightened and she tried to focus on breathing until it tightened to the last squeeze and Faith held her breath. Three seconds went by and the Nurse let her grip on the pump go and the puffed-up cuff on her arm released a long sigh of air.

"Okay, a little high, but not too bad." The Nurse told her the stack of numbers as if Faith were a nursing student and could understand them. She had no idea what that fraction meant even when it was good. Faith only knew what one set of numbers meant, the numbers on the scale.

"Is your blood pressure normally running high? Some people are just on the high side," the Nurse asked while charting the numbers and trying to make Faith feel better.

"Um, no, I don't think so, maybe I'm just a little anxious today." Once Faith said the word "anxious," her hands immediately agreed flushing her palms with warmth.

"Nervous for your appointment?" the Nurse asked as she motioned for her to step up on the Children's Hospital scale.

Faith couldn't tell her everything she was nervous about, starting with that large scale. She was nervous about what questions the doctors would ask her that day. She was nervous that when they examined her and pressed on her belly that they would be able to feel everything that was still wrong with her. She was nervous that she might show pain in her face when they pressed on her stomach and asked her if it felt tender in any areas. She was nervous that she might slip and tell the doctor that it still hurt all over and it hurt as bad as it did the day she first came to the Hospital.

She was nervous that she might not be able to lie convincingly when she told them she only felt like a "pain 3" smiley face.

But what she was most nervous about, at every outpatient appointment, was that they would find too many things wrong with her to let her go home again.

She couldn't let that happen.

Not again.

But there was one thing she didn't have to lie about today.

There was one thing that kept her teetering on the edge of outpatient care, not quite falling into the abyss of inpatient care.

There was no bleeding that day.

At least she didn't have to lie about that.

She was still broken, she just wasn't bleeding out life at that moment.

But she knew, even on those days, that it was only the smallest of victories. She knew that there would eventually be more tests and more medicine. There would always be more tests and more medicine. She just didn't want that for today. For one day, she just wanted to feel like she was moving forward instead of backward.

She just wanted to feel less broken than she actually was.

Makenzie

"How did your appointment go, did they give you any new meds or tell you anything new?" Makenzie rushed through every word, running them together just to hear Faith's answer quicker.

"Yeah it went alright I guess . . . nothing new, just made sure I'm taking the medicine and aren't having any flare-ups right now." Faith sighed loudly, "Took enough blood from me to warrant another blood transfusion though, you know, the usual"

"Okay and so how much did you weigh? Did they say anything? Was it okay?"

"Oh yeah, I weighed just a little over one hundred pounds, like one hundred point three I think."

"Dude, that's great! So since you gained weight they didn't say anything then, right?" Makenzie felt a victory for Faith's world where gaining weight was exciting.

"Well they said they expected me to gain like five to ten pounds by now. I guess most people on the steroids when the medicine is working start to gain weight really fast . . . like they gain five pounds in their face alone he said . . . so he was stuck on that for a while, but he said because I was so sick it might just take longer for me to gain weight back. He said as long as I wasn't losing weight that the medicine must be working okay. But the medicine doesn't work! It's like they know there isn't a cure but they just want to always be doing all these tests and trying new medicines and I don't want that, I just don't want to keep doing that . . . Oh my God, can you imagine though if I didn't eat so much and hadn't tried to gain weight, they probably would have admitted me right back in the Hospital. Thank God . . ."

"Yeah, Thank God! And baby Jesus, and Mother Mary, the whole damn clan of holiness!" Makenzie said, rethinking in her mind the value of bacon fat while knowing that although it helped this time that cured-meat wasn't a cure for Faith's disease.

{There was no cure.}

Faith

Grandma asked Faith how she was feeling that day, and Faith thought for just a second about the truth. She was okay. She had pain but it was a normal amount of pain. To her, any pain would be normal. When she really thought about it, it wasn't that bad of a day. And once she admitted it, her Grandma was excited, "Oh good! I'm so glad you're feeling better!"

But it wasn't that exciting to Faith, because feeling better wasn't getting better. And immediately after she said she was doing okay, she wanted to recant it. She wasn't really feeling better, she just didn't happen to be curled up in a ball of pain wishing for death at that moment. It was just that day she felt less bad; it wasn't a promise for the next day to feel okay. It wasn't the flu she was getting over, it was a disease that she'd have forever.

She'd take the good days for what they were, but she knew to deflect the overjoyed responses that everyone had for her good days.

Everything could change at any time.

And she couldn't ever be glad that they were glad about it.

And she certainly couldn't tell them about her upcoming bad days or they'd think she was a pessimist. Maybe she was, but it was the truth. This disease would never leave her. It might give her a good day or maybe a good month but it would cycle back and she knew it. Even her best days didn't mean that she was shitting rainbows and butterflies yet, even the best days could still end with her rocking back and forth on a bathroom floor.

But she couldn't tell people that, because they wouldn't understand.

They were her truths to deal with.

All her painful truths.

Makenzie

"Fay . . . I have to tell you something." Makenzie had been marinating in disappointment long enough, and it was time she finally shared it with somebody. She looked down at her hands in her lap, and looked up quickly to continue, "Don't be mad, okay?" Makenzie's voice trailed off as she winced remembering the dead arm that Faith had given her the day she told her about smoking her first cigarette. She remembered how disappointed and mad Faith was. And she knew that this would be worse, because Faith was still mad at Makenzie for her first cigarette every time she lit one in front of her.

Makenzie knew this would be much worse because of how hard it was to bring the words up now. Makenzie could skillfully bring ice cream back up right after eating it without getting a brain freeze. She could bring up mashed potatoes and gravy through her nose. She could bring up fried food almost still intact without choking. But these words that were dying to come out, were the hardest to spit up right now.

Makenzie's hands started to shake in her lap, trembling as if they were the cause of her heart pounding like a drumroll introducing the words she was about to unveil.

"Alright, I won't be mad, I promise, what is it?" Faith shook her head squinting her eyes and looking Makenzie up and down. Makenzie knew what Faith's eyes were scanning her for.

"Did you . . . ?" Faith's eyes got big. She had made Makenzie promise her when they were twelve that she wouldn't have sex just because her friends were. She remembered Faith yelling at her in their room at Grandma's and making Makenzie middle-finger-swear that she would wait until she was for real in love. She knew that's what Faith was asking now, and maybe she'd be relieved that it wasn't that kind of confession.

"No, it's not about the V-card, don't worry." Makenzie watched Faith's eyes lower back to their normal size.

"Oh good, it can't be that bad then, what is it . . . ?" Faith questioned.

"Ok. I don't want to tell you this, but I have to . . ." Makenzie looked down again and her eyebrows lifted. "Um . . . well . . . okay." Tears were coming before words. Makenzie choked back emotion and tried to pull forward vowel sounds. She was constantly in a fight to keep things down and bring things up. She just wanted it all to end. And she knew that saying it out loud would make it real, but that it would also make it easier to recover. Once she claimed it, she would own it. And once she owned it, it would no longer have so much control over her.

She just needed help getting control. She knew that she had to tell someone. And she knew that she could tell Faith anything. She knew that even though Faith would be mad, that she would try to understand her. But if it was this hard to tell Faith, she especially knew she couldn't tell anyone else. Because she knew that the associated reaction after anyone admitted that they have an eating disorder is for people to tell them to stop. That they're "beautiful the way they are," and all that bullshit. But eating disorders aren't always about self-image. Sometimes they are just about self-worth. And patchy self-worth can't just be covered up with makeup. She loved herself, a lot.

But it wasn't enough.

She couldn't love herself enough to make up for all the times that other people made her feel unloved. She couldn't stop wanting more. And that's what she tried to fill herself with. And that's what she had to purge.

Makenzie felt nauseated just thinking about it now.

Maybe it meant the words were close to coming out.

"What!? Tell me!" Faith's voice was rising and Makenzie's heartbeat was in her throat.

Makenzie drew a big sigh, deeply filling her gut with air and hoping the words would just be released on their own without her having to push each one out.

"There's a lot of times . . . where I just feel so sick . . ." Makenzie took another breath to pull courage, "that I make myself throw up." Makenzie opened up her hands in her lap as if she were giving Faith something.

She was giving her the biggest secret she had.

"Like . . . when you're sick and you feel like you'd feel better if you just threw up already . . . ?"

Faith looked like she remembered feeling like that when she had the flu and her eyes were searching for what kind of confession this was. She didn't get it. Or maybe she just wanted Makenzie to admit it out loud.

To say the words.

To claim it.

"Yeah, but . . . I do it . . . after I eat." Makenzie looked away to the farthest corner of the room feeling guilty for all the times that she had left Faith after meals to retreat to the bathroom and how many times she had come out of the bathroom with a tissue. She remembered all the times Faith would see her watery eyes and ask if she was okay, if she had been crying, and all the times Makenzie had lied to her, ignoring her worries, and how she had made an excuse for her watery eyes and flushed face, that she had just sneezed or just yawned.

And when Makenzie glanced back at Faith for her reaction, Faith just looked hurt. She looked devastated. This was different from the time that Makenzie had told her about cigarettes and every cigarette she smoked afterward. All those times, Faith was just outwardly frustrated. This time, this time was different, Faith looked hurt all the way in. She looked like she was broken inside in a way that Makenzie had never seen her show before.

Faith shook her head and her voice cracked, slowly spilling out words, "What the fuck . . . Makenzie . . . ?"

"I'm sorry . . ." Makenzie didn't realize how much hurting herself would hurt Faith. She didn't want to carry the secret anymore, but she didn't want to weigh Faith down with it either.

"But . . . why do you it? Is this something your stupid friends are doing?" Faith sounded like all of the air had been let out of her. She sounded exhausted with the idea of bulimia. She only knew Makenzie's school friends well enough to call them stupid when there were cigarettes, sex, and potential disorders involved, but this wasn't about her friends. It was just something inside of her that wouldn't stop.

"What is it? Some kind of girls' locker room club?! You don't need to do that, it's not you, Mazie, you're smarter than that!"

Faith erupted with the disappointment Makenzie had anticipated. She knew there would be some. There had to be at least a little, but of course Faith threw in encouragement—"you're smarter than that"—which was different than calling someone stupid. It was just letting her know that she didn't have to fall into this. But Faith didn't know how deep Makenzie had already fallen. She should have told her weeks ago, but she didn't want to admit herself that it had become a weekly routine.

"No! Nobody knows that I do this, I don't like it either okay . . ." Makenzie felt more ashamed of herself then than if she had really just lost her virginity. Giving herself up to someone, even a stranger, would have left her with more self-worth than she had now.

"Then what the fuck? Why do you think you have to do that, do you think you're fat or something?" Faith shook her head and rubbed her forehead trying to get to the root of the problem.

"No . . . I mean, not really." Makenzie was searching for feelings that she couldn't describe. Makenzie knew how she looked. She wasn't perfect but she was cute, she even felt sexy sometimes. And she liked more things about herself than she hated. This wasn't about beauty. It was about pain. And the thing is, is that people can't see pain. Especially past beauty.

Even worse, they don't understand it.

"Then what is it?! Why do you do that?"

Faith looked how a parent feels when their kids disappoints them.

"I don't know why I do it . . . I just feel so sick after I eat and it makes me feel better." Makenzie tried to convince Faith and herself that the act of purging really did make her feel better. But it didn't. It never did.

"Cause you eat too much at once?" Faith was quick to suggest. As if the answer to the problem could be as simple as telling her not to do that. Just don't eat so much.

"Not that . . . sometimes I throw up when I haven't even eaten much of anything at all, and it hurts so bad those times . . . it's just acid and . . ."

"Then why the hell do you do it?!" Faith waved her hand and jerked her head as if drawing a giant question mark in the air.

Faith didn't understand. And Makenzie couldn't explain it to her, because she didn't really know how it started either. She just felt sick all the time. She knew that vomiting was basically the worst feeling in the world, and could see how doing it voluntarily over and over again would seem like a crazy-dumb-thing to do. She knew that.

"I don't know. I feel sick, so I throw up to feel better, it just . . . I can't explain it but it's just what I have to do. It's how I control my feelings."

"If you can control it, then why don't you just stop . . . ?"

Faith looked at Makenzie with hopeful eyes and Makenzie wished that the bulimia never existed. She wished it were just that easy.

She wished that she could control it without it controlling her.

But, the truth was, it was already out of control.

Faith

Bulimia.

Faith hated that word. It didn't have a hard fatal sound to it like "Anorexia" did, but instead it sounded like the exact act it described. The word itself, "Bulimia" purged vowels off the tongue and vomited out of the mouth as it was said.

Makenzie hadn't used the word yet, but they both knew that's what it was. And they knew what it meant. But Faith wanted to understand it more. She needed to understand it better in a way that she could help Makenzie. So she searched every website she could find from chat forums, to blogs, to help centers to learn why people find themselves stuck in bulimia cycles, and how to really get out.

Faith felt less defeated and more hopeful with every Google search she did.

Makenzie would get better. There were plenty of ways to get better. There were people who survived this and she knew Makenzie would too.

"I looked up a lot of stuff on bulimia, I guess it really is like an addiction, like a disease. Some of the sites say it's like a brain chemical thing, like how anxiety is. Some of the sites say it's coded in genetically too . . . like you'll be more prone to it if your parents have anxiety and that sort of stuff." Faith's voice was pausing as she read through the internet articles, reporting back to Makenzie on the other end of the phone, "So it's not really your fault that you feel this way. I know you don't want to feel this way. And I don't want you to get upset at yourself and stress yourself out about it. That won't help anything, and I get that. It's just now we have to try really hard to face it, and to work through it. I think stress is a big thing with it. We just have to try to not let you get stressed out." Faith took a deep breath. Makenzie took a deep breath in as Faith exhaled loudly.

"We will just have to take it day by day and try to get you through it okay, I got a lot of good info from the one site on coping and recovery . . . and it'll be okay. We got this."

"What if nothing helps it? What if I'm like this forever?"

Makenzie panicked through the phone and Faith wished that she were there to give her a hug just then to re-assure her that it would all be okay.

Makenzie sounded overpowered. "I don't want to be this fucked up! I just want to be normal. I hate feeling like this, Fay! I hate it . . ."

"You'll be okay, if it ever would get too bad there are places, like special retreats and rehabs you can go to that help with this with therapy and things. You don't have to worry, one way or another you'll be okay. I promise it'll all be okay. You're way stronger than you think. And I'm going to help you. Bulimia has nothing on us."

"Thanks, Fay . . ." Makenzie sounded hopeful.

"It's not just you," Faith said. "This happens to so many other people."

"Yeah . . ." Makenzie shifted the weight of her voice.

"And you're not in it alone. You're never alone, okay?" Faith grabbed Makenzie's hand through the phone in her mind, and she squeezed it tightly.

"Thank you, Faith. I don't know what I'd do without you . . ." Makenzie sighed.

"You'd be a mess without me, we both know it," Faith teased, "I'm just kidding."

"It's true though, Fay!" Makenzie sighed.

Faith, having eight different Google tabs open on her computer, was still reading about bulimia, "So, this is crazy . . . here it says that ninety-five percent of the body's serotonin is made in your gut. That's what we're learning about in psychology class now, it's the "feel good hormone" and its main gig is to make you happy. . . . This is crazy though, I thought because serotonin was a magic-neurotransmitter-thingy that it only lived in your brain—but it's in your guts . . ."

"Weird . . ." Makenzie tried to agree, but Faith wasn't sure she was making the same discovery she was and Faith broke it down for Makenzie:

"That literally means that when you throw up,
        you're throwing away all of your happiness."

The idea of control will ruin you.
It will anger you.
        It will tear you apart.
                It will take over if you let it.
But you can't.
It's just an idea.
Control doesn't really exist.

You have to stop telling yourself that you could have changed what happened and that you somehow can change what is happening now.

You couldn't.
No one could.
It was, and it still is out of your control.
It doesn't mean that you're out of control.
        You're fine.

If Heaven were here, she would tell you that.
That this was how it had to be.
That nothing you did could have changed anything.
And that being angry and blaming yourself for not being able to control the past or the future is only going to hurt worse. If you keep thinking like this, you will only be re-inventing pain.

Heaven would tell you that it's just a little rain.
        And it's not the rain that kills you,
                it's the pain of wanting to control the sun.

. . . .

I tell the people in the room about the things that need planned, while the discussion of it has launched a feeling of betrayal deep in my stomach.

My stomach is seizing as the words are coming out.

I can't help but feel that we should have planned life better before all this.
We should have made better plans.
Before planning for her death.
And now I'm crying again at all that I should have done.

And I start to think about what might have saved her.

In my old life, the one that ended 3 days ago, I heard people say before that love is patient, love is kind, and that love is all you need. But those people, the Bible, and the Beatles are all wrong. Because love is never enough. All I can think about right now is how much I love her. And it's this thought that makes me cry hard all over again. She had no idea how many people loved her. If love could have saved her, I know she would have never left.
But love couldn't save her.
And even though I can't stop wanting it to, it can't bring her back either.

I will love her forever. I already knew that, but now I can feel it. I can feel how even though she's gone that my love for her is still there. And I can still feel her love for me. It still exists. She won't ever tell me again, but I can feel it around me right now.
And that's how I know that Heaven exists.
Because I can feel it.

I can still feel all her love. All of it. She may be gone but it's not. And I let out the weight of wondering what could have saved her in a sigh. I reach for the notebook with the peach cover and my pen, and I write,

"Hey Best Friend,
Member how you used to always say that neither of us could both be sad at the same time? That no matter what, one of us always needed to be happy to balance the other one, like a see-saw? You were right. You were always right. We were yin and yang and I remember you used to ask me and make sure I was happy before admitting that you were sad about something. And that's how I know now. I know that you've got to have all the happiness of Heaven. Because it was your rule. We can't both be sad. And I'm just glad that you'll never have to go through this Hell. I'm glad you're so happy that you're probably shitting rainbows right now. . . . I love you more than corn muffins at 3am . . ."

And while I'm writing, I hear someone in the room talking as though they know the point in history that if only one thing was changed, it would have stopped this all from happening. But that person is wrong. Because that thought is a bigger mistake than anything. It's a mistake I can't un-do. And now my thoughts are taking the journey of the words from this room. And now, I too am trying to go back and imagine how things, if changed, could have ended differently. Or just not ended at all.

But I can't think about those things.
I can't change this.
And it's the hardest thought that I don't know how to accept. This cannot be changed.
The past cannot be changed.
And now, the future cannot be *un-changed.*

Thinking of the future brings my body to trembling.

I can't stop feeling like I need to see her right now.
In front of me.
And the only way I'll ever be able to again, is in photos.
I need to see her alive again.

And now, the thought of it is consuming me. I need to find every photo that she's ever been in, and I need to share them all. I don't know why I need to prove to everyone that she was alive. That she lived.

I need to see the proof.

So I interrupt their conversation about the past and I tell everyone what we need to do. I ask the friends in the room to get poster board, tape, and frames, and I tell them that I will get all the pictures. They nod their heads. They are happy to have something to help with, "anything" they say.

But when I grab my keys, everyone in the room turns bi-polar. They freak. They look at each other for backup. Each set of eyes in the room is urging the next set of eyes to say something, to be the one to stop me.

"I'm fine," I say, "I'll be fine, I'm just going to go to my Grandma's and get some pictures, and I'll be back."

But they don't want to let me leave, or drive, or probably die.

They're all looking at me like they can't let me go.

But I need to go.

I need to find her.

Makenzie

The first time she met him she had already been waiting for him her whole life, or at least the last two weeks.

He had dark brown hair that was almost black. The sides of his head were awkwardly shaved-to-the-skin-clean and he had a tall mohawk with a red tip.

She was beautiful with anticipation. Her hair was freshly cut and styled and her strawberry blonde hair was dyed bright-rock-star-pink at the ends.

Anyone who saw them would have known that they were perfect for each other, but no one would have understood it at all.

They were outside, finally, away from the warm smell of sweat and beer that all concerts inside a building held. The fresh air felt cool against Makenzie's face; she took a deep breath, able to breathe now without taking in the smell of strangers. She was nervous. She was more nervous now than she was skipping her last two classes that day to get an appointment at the salon in time for the concert. She was more nervous now than she was picking at and ripping chicken nuggets apart in the McDonald's booth trying to force food in on the way up to the concert when Faith and the girl with the tattoos asked her if all she was really going to eat was the layer of skin off the chicken nuggets.

She was more nervous now, waiting for him.

Knowing that he would be there any second.

She looked at Faith to see any indication of when he would be there. But no one was looking, no one was waiting like she was.

Groups of strangers erupted loudly from the building, funneling people into the parking lot where Makenzie was standing.

Makenzie, Faith, and the girl with the tattoos stood together with a small group of friends. They all stood still like cogs in the gears of groups of people moving all around.

And then it happened.

He came up behind her taking large strides in his sloppily tied combat boots and blue camo cargo pants. He wore an opened black leather jacket with chains hanging from it and a red and black plaid shirt that peeked out to her from the leather of his jacket with each step he took towards her.

He didn't walk like most boys Makenzie knew in school, he didn't walk to make it look like he had swag. He didn't need his walk to do that, you could tell by looking at him. He walked straight towards her, without hesitation and in that moment Makenzie realized what her years of braces were for, remembering how when she first got them how much she had cried and cried. How that first entire week she had to have her Grandmother liquefy food for her in the blender. How every meal once blended tasted just like mashed potatoes and gravy.

Now she knew that her Brace Face served a purpose.

Pain and embarrassment now made sense.

It was all leading up to this moment.

To have the perfect smile for him.

And Makenzie's red lipstick stretched to frame her beautiful perfect teeth.

His eyes were locked on her as if he wasn't moving through a crowd of people bumping and crossing paths.

He walked closer to her and only feet away she could already tell that he was the perfect height. The exact equation of her height plus heels would equal the perfect kiss with him, and it wasn't too ridiculous to imagine their first kiss before they even officially met, not to Makenzie.

He was inches away and she could smell his cologne. It was sweet smelling in a manly way.

His face was serious in a quirky way and he stretched out long arms to her. She wondered if she should get ready for a hug, but he quickly grabbed her by the tops of her shoulders, locking his arms and keeping a wide gap between them.

Makenzie's smile turned to a confused grin.

He parted his lips to say "You're Makenzie." With a slight shake to her shoulders, he introduced himself with another small jolt, and said "and I'll be right back." With one final serious grasp on her shoulders and a smile that never broke until he left.

Makenzie was still staring, literally shaken by his introduction.

It was like nothing she had planned in her head.

It was so much better.

It was perfect.

She needed a minute to breathe.

She smiled and looked around for proof that what had just happened was real. No version of meeting him that she had pre-planned in her head had prepared her for this. She even had a plan for what she would have done if he would have walked up and kissed her. There was a plan for that, but not this.

"Fay . . ." Makenzie's arms were still tight at her side as if they were afraid to move until he came back.

"Urgh . . . I saw . . ." Faith made an awful face, and sounded disgusted, ". . . that hair, I had no idea, he must have just done that, sorry."

"No, Fay! Did you *see* that . . . ?" Makenzie's red lips were fixed in an awestruck shape and her arms were still at her sides. Her arms would have waited the rest of her life for him to come back.

He was tall.

He was mysterious.

He was unmistakably meant for her.

Plus, he totally had a mohawk.

Faith

She never wanted Makenzie to meet him. She wanted to protect her from the whole male population, especially ones like him.

He was the single worst thing any man could be.

He was charming.

Faith's cell phone rang as she was just getting home from school. She answered, "Hey, Happy Birthday!" she waited for a thank you on the other end but instead there was a half-whisper-yell from Makenzie.

"Faith . . . ! Guess what?"

"Uhhh . . . I dunno," but Faith knew the guessing meant it had to be something good, otherwise Makenzie would have just spilled it.

"Dude, I just came home and my dad said that there were people at the door looking for me . . ."

Faith thought maybe she was wrong about the good nature of the news and guessed, "Like . . . police officers . . . ?"

"No, like kids from school, and he said how stupid looking my friends were. But Fay, my friends would never come knock on the door. Never. They don't even step on the lawn I mean they know that if . . ."

"Yeah . . . so . . ."

"Faith!" Makenzie couldn't believe that Faith didn't guess it, "It was him!"

"Who?" Faith asked. Of course Makenzie wanted it to be the boy with the mohawk more than anything but Faith didn't think it was him.

"And like two of his friends I guess." Makenzie ignored her question.

"Are you sure? He doesn't even know where you live . . ." Faith was almost positive she wouldn't have disclosed where Makenzie lived to him, even if by accident.

"We were talking about how we both lived in New Castle. I said my house was across from the golf course with the red shutters!" Makenzie sounded like she was reminding Faith of a conversation that she was never in but should have remembered.

"Oh." Faith was confused, maybe it was him.

"And when my dad said about how weird my friends were he said '*who even has a mohawk these days*'! He had a mohawk, Fay!" Makenzie sounded like she was jumping up and down on the other side of the phone.

"Oh God, you didn't tell your dad that they were my weird friends did you?" Faith was more worried now than when she thought the police were at Makenzie's door.

"Well, yeah, but, Fay! Don't you get it!? He came by to wish me a happy birthday! He came to my house. Knocked on my front door. Met my fucking dad. On my birthday. Because he remembered!"

"How did he know it was your birthday?" Faith was wondering how he knew so much about Makenzie from their one date.

"He remembered from the concert! I said we were there because you bought me tickets for my 16th birthday and he said "happy birthday" and I said that it won't be my birthday until the fifteenth. He fucking remembered like two weeks later and just showed up at my house!"

"Wow. That's crazy." Faith was thinking maybe she didn't know the boy with the mohawk that well because she would not have expected him to go to Makenzie's house and meet her dad. She looked around her bedroom, looking for something that she was obviously missing. At least he didn't bring her a present, or flowers, or a card, Faith thought.

"And guess what I found when I came upstairs?!"

Oh no, Faith thought, please not a present, and was afraid to even ask ". . . What?"

Makenzie laughed as if it were an inside joke that they were both sharing for the zillionth time, "He didn't like call you right after he did this? Fay, this is hilarious!"

"No, what is it?" Faith wished that he would have really called her to run these things by her, she wished she could have deflected this whole situation.

"It took me awhile to see it, but . . ."

"What!?" Faith couldn't stand being the only one who didn't know what was going on.

"Across the street,
        On the edge of the golf course,
              Behind the tree,
                    Drawn in the sand,
                          Is a giant . . .
                                Penis."

"A what now?" Faith lowered her voice in the exact opposite direction of the excitement that Makenzie had about the situation.

"A PENIS! They drew a giant penis in the sand trap!" Makenzie was elated.

"Oh god . . ."

"I know, isn't that the funniest thing you've ever heard?" Makenzie couldn't stop laughing.

"You've got to erase it. Right now." Faith was serious, if it weren't the cops knocking on Makenzie's door earlier they would surely link her to the penis in the sand crime later. Defacing private property and trespassing on the country club golf course, she'd be in for it then.

"No, he drew it for me! It's funny, c'mon, a phallic symbol in the middle of a sand trap at the most prestigious country club in town. Those old men will have a heart attack when their ball goes in this pit and they see a giant penis. When their balls go into the penis pit. . . . C'mon that's hilarious!" Makenzie laughed, "And besides I already checked, no one can see it from the road or even the sidewalk, you can only see it from above, from my window! It's because I told him which room was mine, he knew I'd be able to see it!"

Great, Faith thought, the exact thing she was trying to protect Makenzie from was now six feet wide and right outside her bedroom window.

"Fay . . ." Makenzie stopped giggling for only a second.
"Yeah?" Faith sighed.
"I fucking love this kid."

The days will move on, but they will come and go differently now. Instead of starting and ending, they will feel like they are just spinning you all around.

Making you dizzy.

But you've got to let the days go where they will take you.

· · · · · · · ·

Alone in the car, I think about how long it took us to shop and pick out outfits for all the concerts we went to. We planned outfits months ahead of time, right down to matching underwear. But now I think about her entire wardrobe and I wonder if she would care as much about the outfit she's going to be wearing for eternity as she would have cared about what she wore out on a Friday night.

I wonder why we've never talked about things like what she would want to wear forever. And I can't stop thinking about "forever." It's such a big word. Kind of like "Heaven."

"Forever" and "Heaven" are grouped together in my mind, but before this I had never thought of Heaven as a bad thing, until I realized that it couldn't get away from "forever." Before now, Heaven had been buy one get one free shoe sales, long weekends, and cute boys. Now, Heaven was none of those things.

Now . . . it was something that took everything away.

Everything is gone.
    She's gone.
        She's already left.
And she can't possibly care about what color the flowers draping over her casket will be or what they will smell like or what her empty shell of a body will being wearing four days after she already left it. These details are about as meaningful to her now as my entire past existence felt to me the minute I found out she was gone.

I think about all of the decisions I thought I had to make a week ago and those thoughts and details are completely and utterly void to me. I actually sat at the McDonald's drive through for five minutes last week deciding what to get for dinner as if the choice between a Big Mac and a Double Cheeseburger were so drastically different and that choosing the wrong one might have fucked up my day.

How naive was I.

Now I'm helping with funeral details and I can see that it's just all the same. I can see how none of the details that we think are important really matter. Sandwich ingredients or colors of roses. It's all the same. My entire existence, past, present, and future were all void in the moment she left. Everything is the same. Nothing can make me believe that any of this Earth business would matter to her in the slightest now.

She's gone.
She's in Heaven.
She's over the planning, and nothing that we do will be so impressive to her that it will bring her back. Death is unmoved by these things.
But we don't have the luxury of discarding them.
And we need the motions of putting something together for her.
Because we are still stuck here.
Still.

And all of these things we are doing—the pictures, the flowers, the music, the finishing touches—are all decorating her life while highlighting her death. It feels like we're trying to wrap a shiny satin bow around the flames of hell, and even though no knot could contain them, I've got to make sure that this bow is the prettiest freaking bow there is, because she deserves it.

She deserves the best.

Faith

"This one's pretty!" Faith jokingly laughed at a sparkly silver sequined dress on the end of the department store rack.

"Eh, too much glitter," Makenzie's eyes widened as if to show how much was "too much." She walked past the rack and gravitated towards the ball gowns, shouting over to her Grandma, "We're going to look over here!"

Faith looked at all of the gowns, shopping only with her eyes while Makenzie pushed hangers back and forth. There were bold colors and designs on every rack in the junior's section. A pale blue fabric suffocating between two bold prints caught Faith's eye and she peeled the dress out to hold it up in front of her.

It was a floor-length Cinderella-blue princess cut spaghetti strap dress with white lace-like flowers in a thin layer of organza over top of it.

"Try it on, Fay!" Makenzie shouted from two racks over, "It's pretty, it looks just like you!"

"I dunno . . . maybe I should just wait . . ." Faith held the dress farther away to look at it.

"Wait for what? We are here now. Looking at dresses. Try it on, dude!"

" . . . Wait until I maybe have a date and actually plan on going to prom for sure before I spend money on a dress."

"You're going. You don't NOT go to prom. It's your Junior Prom! You know I would kill to go to prom this year!" Makenzie made a funny face as she walked past Faith to another rack of fluffy and sequined gowns.

"Alright, well you try one on with me then." Faith took the pale blue dress that she was about to say goodbye to a minute ago and now thanks to Makenzie tucked it under her arm.

Makenzie scanned the rack of gowns for a red one and she found the brightest lipstick shade of gown there was. Makenzie tucked it under her arm and the tiny girls lugged the long dresses back to the dressing rooms.

Their Grandma waited outside the dressing room as the girls tried on their dresses. Faith came out just far enough outside the dressing room for her grandmother to see her and Faith did a little twirl in the pale blue dress. Makenzie came out with her bright red ball gown on and walked the carpet between the dressing rooms like it were a runway during Fashion Week. The body of the dress opened at the bottom like a true rose, hugging at her hips and then gently flowing out before the bottom of the dress came back under to kiss the ground. She looked like a model even without the walk; even Makenzie's nail polish matched the dress.

Makenzie couldn't stop laughing at how the dress made her feel.

"Oh my gosh!" Faith gasped and ran back into her dressing room to grab her phone.

"What are you doing? Here, let me take a picture of you, it's your prom!" Makenzie reached for Faith's phone.

"No! I have to take a picture of you!" Faith held her rectangular cell phone firm, "You need to see how beautiful you look."

Makenzie laughed as if she didn't believe Faith but blushed as if part of her did. She confidently struck a pose with her right hand on her hip and her left arm stretched high, leaning on the open doorway of the dressing room and she smiled a crooked smile, only crooked because her lips were trying hard to keep from laughing.

And Faith's phone mocked the sound of a real camera, *chick*.

Makenzie

"Hey, I'm going to try on my dress to show Grandpa," Faith giggled as she slowly pulled out her dress from the closet in their room at their Grandma's house and took it off the only hanger it had ever lived on.

Faith peeled away the thin clear plastic that covered the dress, carefully as if anything she did would wrinkle it.

Faith undressed, stepped carefully into the dress, and Makenzie zipped her up in the back thinking about how only the most serious of occasions called for the zipper to be in the back of the dress instead of the side. Occasions that require help with not just zippers but nerves too. Makenzie wished that she could have at least one back-zipper moment in her future. She let out a little sigh thinking about how she had been invited to the prom by the boy with the mohawk, but her dad and stepmom wouldn't let her go. They said it was because she was only a sophomore. Sophomores didn't need to go to the prom, they shouldn't go, they said. And when she had told them about the other 10th grade friends she knew going to the prom, they had said that the only sophomores that get invited to the prom are sluts.

Sluts.

She didn't get how they could say that about her.

Is that really what they thought about high school, or what they really thought about her? How could the only reason someone would want to be around her was if she was slutty, when she wasn't even an ounce of slutty.

Did they really think that badly about her?

Or did they just want her to think that badly about herself?

Maybe they just didn't want to shell out the money for a dress, or spoil her for one goddamn day of her life. Maybe having the attention on her for one day would be too much, maybe the thought of someone else appreciating her company would mean that they were wrong, that she wasn't the second class citizen they treated her as.

Makenzie watched as Faith floated out the doorway looking lighter than she had in the past few months. It felt so good to see Faith in a real gown instead of a hospital gown. Faith's sloppy folded ponytail and bare feet in the dress made Makenzie smile. She thought she'd better ask Faith what shoes she was wearing with the dress when she came back into the room or Faith might not think of a thing like that.

More than that she should ask her what she's doing with her hair.

And her nails.

And her makeup.

Better yet . . .

Makenzie better just make sure she's there to help her get ready for the dance.

She knew Faith never thought of stuff like that.
Plus she wanted to be there to see her off.

Heaven left a hole in your heart.

But it's up to you to choose if that hole will be filled with pain, anger, and the eternal darkness of loss . . .
Or if you will choose to fill it with light and love and have that hole shine out of you like a spotlight into your life, keeping their memory alive . . .

{It's up to you.}

. . . .

For days now people have kept telling me that I need to eat like if I don't eat that very moment, that I will forget how to entirely. I won't forget how to eat, I just don't want to. And it's more than that, I simply can't eat.

I can't do it.

But they don't understand. I can see it in their eyes that they don't understand that thinking about food, just the thought of food to me right now, is comparable to asking me to drink water from a cement mixer.

It's impossible.

The people from the house that isn't mine tried coaxing food to me for the past few days like I were a child and it were a prize, and they've tried forcing it on me while freaking out about how I haven't eaten anything yet. Saying "yet" and marking time as starting from the moment that she left.

But I still feel like that's when time ended.

And all the people trying to feed me didn't want to say it, but I could see that their faces were all tense with the responsibility to keep me alive now.

I'd go on a hunger strike until I were dead if it would bring her back. But there's something about how she didn't come back already that tells me that it would be useless. And part of me wants to submit to the idea of death by starvation, if it meant that I could see her again soon.

And I think about her.
And what she would say . . .

She would beg me to eat.

Only because my Grandma is the one asking me now and she has heartbroken eyes as we sit at her dining room table in her yellow and blue kitchen, do I shrug my shoulders and say "alright" to her pleas for me to eat a sandwich. At least if I try to eat something here, now, I can tell the others tonight to calm down when I get back to the house that isn't mine. I'll be able to tell them that I've already eaten something today. They won't know how much, but eating a bite or two of sandwich now might save me from having to try to eat again later.

I feel good about the plan to have two swallows under my belt, until I see my Grandma carrying the sandwich, cut in half, over to me on a familiar plate. I recoil. It looks so big, so daunting. There's roast beef spilling out between hamburger buns. One half of it looks like something I just can't handle. Even the sesame seeds that have fallen off the top of the bun on to the plate look like too much for me to eat right now.
It's all too much.
It looks scary.
It looks awful.
{I tell her "Thank you."}

And I stare at the sandwich as it sits in front of me. Hating it. I put my elbows on the table surrounding the sandwich and I rub the side of my temples hard as if to ignite the focus I need to try to eat this. I know that this shouldn't be this hard.
But everything is harder now.

It's on familiar bread on a familiar plate in a familiar kitchen but it all feels so out of place. I never thought one day, one week, one stupid sandwich could take away all of the warm and comfortable memories this kitchen had.
Death stains everything.

I pick up the sandwich half closest to me and hold it in my hands. I hold it by my fingertips, careful not to let my palms touch the sandwich or I'm afraid they might smash it into a ball and throw it across the room. And I try to pretend like none of this is happening and it's just a regular day eating a regular lunch at Grandma's house but my imagination could never stretch so far as to forget her.

So I take a small bite of the sandwich and I think about how she would want me to eat and to be strong and healthy.

And I chew.
 And I chew
 And I swallow.

My Grandma sits down next to me, watching me chew tiny bites and her eyes are waiting with hope like she's watching little birds fly into her backyard to eat the crusts of her morning toast.

Until she brings her hands up to the base of her neckline, just touching her fingertips to the chain of her gold cross, and she looks apologetically to me as she says in a misty whisper, "I don't have anything to wear . . ." and she starts to cry.

It's nothing to cry over, but I know what she means. She means she doesn't own dark depressing clothing that's fit for summer weather. She means that she doesn't own anything appropriate to say goodbye to her in.
 Me neither.

"I don't have anything to wear either, Grandma, we can go to the mall and we'll find something together."

Her eyes are teary but relieved again.

I take another small bite of the roast beef sandwich and something about it, or this moment, or this whole life just makes my mouth pause and my tongue hold on to the bite instead of chew it. My mouth waters around the bite and I feel a reflex. Bursts of tears are coming out for no good reason and so I cover my mouth with my left hand and my eyes widen as if they could stretch to help cover my mouth too. I take a breath from behind my hand and I don't want to but there's a feeling in my stomach that makes me realize how closely the feeling of sorrow matches regret.

I spit out the piece of food before my body has a chance to gag and I wipe my tears with a napkin covered in crumbs. I push the plate away from me, and I grab for my only distraction from the flooding pain. I open up my notebook, turning to the next blank page.

"Hey Best Friend,

Yesterday I went with your mom to pick out the outfit that you will wear for your big day. Your mom actually picked it out and paid for it, I just agreed that it was beautiful. It's a white gown and it's flowing. You'll blend in perfectly with the other angels. It was $80 at the mall, just in case anyone in Heaven asks where you got it from and how much it was. . . . I'm just kidding, I know Heaven isn't like High School, no one will give a flying fuck about how much money was spent or what you're wearing. Heaven doesn't care about Earth matters, it's all water under the bridge, right? But you will look beautiful. . . . You'll never be anything but beautiful."

Makenzie

Makenzie paced Faith's room waiting for her to get home. The girl with the tattoos sat on Faith's bed, waiting to be the photographer for the event. Makenzie had everything from makeup to nail polish ready to help Faith get ready for the prom, but they were running out of time. Faith's date would soon be there to pick her up, and Makenzie had to make sure that no detail was ignored.

When Faith ran upstairs to her room, Makenzie was armed with her mascara in one hand and her eyelash curler in the other.

"What took so long!?" Makenzie rushed Faith into the room.

"Urgh I know! It's just curls I don't know why they took so long doing my hair, this is why I never get my hair done. Oh well, does it at least look okay?" Faith moved her head around Makenzie to peek in the mirror.

"Especially if he does pick you up in his motorcycle, then you'll be real glad you spent so much time getting your hair done," the girl with the tattoos said sarcastically while looking out Faith's bedroom window, waiting to see what the boy with the motorcycle would drive up on. She was watching, ready to signal to the girls like the Paul Revere of the Prom; one if by motorcycle, two if by Land Rover.

"I don't care, I hope he does come in the motorcycle . . ." Faith smirked.

Makenzie wished the opposite, she didn't want to have to worry about Faith any more than she already did and that included worrying about how Faith's hair would survive helmet head before the prom.

"Let's just hurry up and get some makeup on you quick." Makenzie reached for Faith.

"It's okay if we don't get everything on, I know we're running out of time. Just need to put on the dress at least," Faith laughed and closed her eyes as Makenzie started applying makeup.

"oh and my purse!" Faith's arms reached out in the direction of her pale blue purse that matched her dress and Makenzie lunged across the room in two steps to grab it and get back to doing her makeup.

"Okay, open your eyes and look at me . . ." Makenzie studied Faith's face and watched her eyes and she blinked, "Perfect!"

"You look beautiful, Fay," The girl with the tattoos turned away from the window to gush at her friend.

"Thanks." Faith smiled and blushed, her cheeks showing how excited she really was.

"Dude! Now let's get the dress on!" Makenzie helped slide Faith's dress over her. She couldn't tell if Faith was more excited about going to prom with her date or about putting on that dress again. Faith had worn the dress almost every Sunday after dinner just to hang out in it. Makenzie straightened out the bottom and zipped up the back for Faith, pulling every piece of fabric into place.

The girl with the tattoos took a picture.

"Are you excited, Fay?!?" Makenzie asked as she clipped the very top hook in place to secure the dress in place.

"Yeah . . . I guess." Faith shrugged her shoulders and smiled.

"I hope you have an awesome time, I can't wait to hear about it!" Makenzie looked at the girl with the tattoos, glad not to be the only one in the room missing prom, even if the girl with the tattoos was un-attending by choice.

"Oh, my shoes!" Faith pointed at her silver strappy shoes across the room, still in the box she bought them in.

"I'll get them." Makenzie grabbed the strappy heels and while Faith was standing in her floor length dress, and because Faith couldn't see her feet, Makenzie helped her step into them one by one.

The girl with the tattoos signaled, he had just pulled up in the Land Rover. Makenzie felt relieved that at least Faith's hair would look perfect all night.

"Oh no, hurry up!" Faith was suddenly way more anxious than she had let on.

"Take your time, I'll run down and talk to him, you know, so he doesn't have to talk to your mom while he waits." The girl with the tattoos snickered and flew down the stairs.

"Ready?" Makenzie asked Faith in a gentle breath as if Faith were about to walk down the aisle instead of just down the steps.

Faith grabbed a tiny glass bottle of perfume from her dresser and spritzed three rose-petal-scented-mists in front of her before twilling through them. "I guess so!" Faith grabbed her purse and gave Makenzie a hug, "Thank you for your help, you know I'd be a mess without you."

"I know you would," Makenzie laughed.

Makenzie followed Faith downstairs to see Faith's date wearing a black suit with a silver tie, holding out his hand for Faith as she came down the stairway. He looked dapper. Of course, there was something about wearing a suit that could make any guy look like the best version of himself.

Faith's mom came in from the kitchen with a zip-lock bag for Faith to put in her tiny clutch and said, "Don't forget your new pills!" before handing off the bag like it were a relay.

"Mom, I'm not taking these with me . . ." Faith rolled her eyes looking embarrassed as if her mom just handed her tampons or condoms in front of her prom date and not medicine.

"Take them with you, and you make sure she takes them." Faith's mom pointed at the boy with the motorcycle as if he was now Faith's babysitter. And Faith's mom and Makenzie proceeded to give Faith's date instructions for taking her out for the night.

Now that she had an incurable disease, she was placed in the same category as babies and old people—fragile.

{Handle with care.}

You'll spend your time grieving all that they were and all that you lost. But in all of the sadness, when you're feeling that your heart is empty, and lacking,

You've got to remember that grief isn't the absence of love.

Grief is the proof that love is still there.

. . . .

We pull up to the mall's parking lot. My Grandma and I take a deep breath before getting out of my car. The car doors slam behind us, and I think of her.

Every sound feels so much louder now, echoing in her absence.

I walk around from the driver's side of the car and like the child that I will forever be now, my hand finds my Grandma's palm like a magnet as if we are at the crossroads of the scariest street in our lives. And in a way, that is exactly where we are.

She holds my hand face up in the parking lot and opens it revealing a metal disk in the center of my palm and asks confused, "What's this?"

"Oh . . ." I peel back the black and silver metal object from my hand that I forgot I was holding on to. It's been pressed against my hand so tight ever since I found it that it's become a part of me. I explain to Grandma what the small piece of metal is and before I switch it to my other palm, she gasps loudly as if I've just sworn in church, and then she clasps the piece of metal back into my hand with hers, squeezing hard against it.

It's my very last piece of her.
And it's in a circle.
It's never-ending.

Her other hand is holding a tissue and it rises to her chest in the exact timing that she lowers her hand that's holding mine to her side.

She looks straight ahead at the mall entrance and through the side of her sunglasses I can see that she's crying. Her eyes don't wander to the ground or to the half a dozen people walking beside of and in front of us. The people around us are happy and hurrying to what they think is important.

They have no idea what is important.

She doesn't bother to look at them and neither do I.

She doesn't turn her head both ways to look for cars as we cross the parking lot.

She just keeps her teary gaze on the doors of the mall and her legs keep moving.

I take a deep breath.

And I try to match my gaze and my stride to hers. I squeeze back on her hand as hard as I can with the piece of small metal between us. My eyes start to leak again, a slow constant supply of tears that each blink has to work hard to wipe away.

Faith

The government curfew for kids under eighteen was 11:00 but at 11:35 on a Saturday night Makenzie sat with Faith on Faith's front porch steps, waiting to go somewhere.

Anywhere.

In another year, when they would be eighteen, they wouldn't have to worry about any government curfew, but they weren't all that worried about it now either.

Faith's knees were bent towards the darkness of the sky, and the step beneath her feet and the one below her butt were as broken as the home they sat in front of. The cement of the steps was rounded at the edges and crumbling. They were the same exact steps that Faith used to sit on waiting for her dad to come home from work when she was little, just so that she was the first one to get to talk to him before her brother grabbed his attention with some kind of sports news.

Faith tried not to think of the steps below her as being the last thing in that house that her dad touched. But she couldn't help it. They were the last thing his feet left.

Makenzie pulled a fresh pack of cigarettes out of her purse and slapped them against her wrist, repeatedly. The sound annoyed Faith but not as much as wondering how many cigarettes Makenzie had smoked since Faith saw her last. Faith thought about when Makenzie first told her that she smoked her first cigarette. Faith gave Makenzie a dead arm like she never knew she could give. It took ten minutes for the feeling to come back into Makenzie's arm that day and left a bruise for a week.

But now Faith knew there were bigger demons to worry about. The cigarettes were the lesser of the two evils, but she still hated Makenzie smoking them.

"C'mon, dude, really?" Faith looked to her left and watched Makenzie unwrapping the outer plastic of the pack.

"I'm just having one while we wait for the boys to pick us up . . ." Makenzie quickly opened the carton and tapped the top of eight cigarette filters like a weird game of duck-duck-goose with her pointer finger before flipping the eighth one upside down. Makenzie pulled one out of the tight pack and rested her box of cigarettes on the lap of her jeans in front of her purse while she lit one.

Faith grabbed the box from her lap.

"Hey!" Makenzie gasped mid-inhale.

Instead of throwing the cigarettes into the neighbor's fenced-in yard like she wanted to, Faith slid back the top of the box and pulled on the ends of two cigarettes, making careful not to pull out Makenzie's "lucky" upside-down cigarette. She knew Makenzie would need that one to make a wish on later.

Makenzie looked at Faith unsure of how exactly to yell at her.

"What, I'm just having two cigarettes while we wait for the boys . . ." Faith mocked Makenzie and reached for the lighter from Makenzie's lap to light them both.

"Why are you smoking two cigarettes at once, that's just ridiculous, and you don't even smoke, Faith!" Makenzie held her own cigarette idle in her hand as she watched to see what Faith would do next.

"Well I figure it's two less cigarettes out of this pack that you can kill yourself with. So maybe I will start smoking. Unless my smoking upsets you? And then well . . . geeze?"

Makenzie gave Faith a shove and shook her head, "Okay, I get it. I get it. I promise this is the last pack I'll buy . . ."

The girls locked eyes.

"Middle finger?" Faith asked in a child-like octave.

"Middle-finger-swear." Makenzie assured her and locked middle fingers with Faith like an adult pinky swear and the girls kissed their hand sealing the promise.

They didn't know a Ford from a Chevy, but the girls knew the exact sound that the engine of the light blue truck the boy with the baseball hat drove, and they could hear it coming a block away. Faith used to hate the sound of a truck coming down her street, it would only make her hope for a second that it was her dad's truck pulling up again, and that maybe he was coming home. Any truck sound would only make her feel stupid. But the sound of the boys pulling up in a truck hurt less, like someone wanted her after all.

As soon as the girls heard it, they both slapped each other with the back of their palm and smiled a "get ready" look. Makenzie piled the contents back into her purse and Faith slid her cell phone into her right back pocket as she stood up.

Four houses up, the truck came in to view.

Three houses up, the truck turned its headlights off.

Two houses up, the truck parked.

And the girls left the broken steps to meet it.

The boy with the mohawk and the boy with the motorcycle stood up in the back of the truck, holding their hands out. Makenzie tossed her purse in and took one step on top of the back tire and with the help of the boy with the mohawk's hand, she took a big step into the bed of the truck. Makenzie wrapped her arms around his neck in a hug before saying "Hi" to the other boys.

Faith followed and reached for the boy with the motorcycle's hand outstretched to her as if she were still wearing her Cinderella-blue prom dress and getting into something other than the back of a beat-up old truck.

He helped her into the truck and Faith could see his smile lit by the streetlights.

Faith smiled back.

"Hey, Snotface!" The boy with the motorcycle whispered and playfully elbowed Faith.

Faith squinted at his endearment but instead of just rolling her eyes she stuck her pointer finger into her nose quickly pulling it out and wiping snot down his cheek, "Who's the *Snotface* now?" Faith giggled.

The boy with the motorcycle tried to look disgusted, but he couldn't stop smiling. He wrapped his arms around Faith picking her up effortlessly and swinging her around the back of the truck pretending that he was going to drop her in retaliation for the snot-kiss.

The boy with the baseball hat was driving, and as the girls settled in he smiled big and asked them, "Are you ready for this?" in a way that made it sound like they shouldn't be.

"Hells yeah!" Makenzie whispered and she walked up the back of the truck bed, her flip-flops gently flapping, to the open window of the truck's cab. The boy with the goatee was sitting shotgun and he held his hand through the back window to say hello to Makenzie, expecting a low-five. Makenzie slapped his hand and squeezed it in excitement and he squeezed back. Faith walked up to the window and slapped the boy with the goatee's hand with a smile.

The boys were late, but they always showed up.
They were the only men in the two girls' lives who had yet to let them down.
And that was exactly what the two girls loved most about them all.

Makenzie

Makenzie looked up at the starlit sky from the back of the traveling baby blue truck bed. The truck bed beneath her had long grooves in it for whatever truck beds need them for, maybe so stuff wouldn't slide around so much. Makenzie's body was still sliding with every turn the boy with the baseball hat made, but her head stayed stuck to the boy with the mohawk's arm. Trees ran in and out of view above her and Makenzie could tell exactly where they were in town by the shapes of the trees and the bends of the road. She drew a slow long breath and watched the stars dance in and out of view from behind the trees.

"Fay, look!" Makenzie tried to reach her head up far enough to whisper-yell over to Faith on the other side of the truck bed, "I just saw a shooting star!" The wind whooshed over Makenzie's face and washed away all the worries from her day. As she made a wish, she felt relieved, even though she knew it was probably just a Google Earth satellite and not really a shooting star. That didn't matter. Believing was all that mattered for wishes to come true.

"Are you serious?! I missed it!" Faith was huddled up with the boy with the motorcycle, he had his arms over her in the bed of the moving truck to keep her warm. The summer air felt so much colder when it was racing over 40 mph at night. Faith pulled away from the boy with the motorcycle, just long enough to shout over to Makenzie, "What'd you wish for?!"

"I can't tell you, or it won't come true!" Makenzie smiled at Faith and then returned her eyes to the sky. She thought about how in that moment life was perfect because it was simple. One truck, a world asleep, and a million stars. Sneaking out and breaking curfew at night was the only time she was glad she wasn't allowed to have a cell phone. No one knew where she was, and she didn't have to feel guilty about avoiding any parent's calls. She didn't feel guilty about anything because she didn't think about anything.

It didn't matter where they were going.

She was just existing.

And in that moment, she was happy.

"Fay, I'm not tired, we don't have to go back anytime soon." Makenzie defensively put in her request far before it was needed. Their night was just getting started. But she wanted to feel as free as the air rolling over her body made her feel for as long as she could. The feeling of not hearing or seeing any other cars on the road and being able to roll through red lights at empty intersections.

It didn't matter where they went that night.

The only thing that mattered was that they kept moving, that they were headed somewhere while the rest of the town was just headed to bed. There was something about being awake at night while everyone was sleeping that made Makenzie feel alive.

"I know, don't worry, we won't." Faith smiled just as the boy with the motorcycle pulled her back closer to him and whispered something in her ear that made them both giggle.

Faith

The sky was calm at 2 am. The moon was almost full and Faith loved those nights the most. The moon lit up the night sky in the exact opposite way of the sun. The sunlight had such an annoying way of spreading the pain of the morning everywhere, it left no place untouched. But at night, she was already over all the pain of the day, physically and mentally.

She was stronger for having the day behind her.

The boy with the motorcycle walked up to the gate of his house. Faith, Makenzie, and the other boys followed quietly behind. "I just want to grab something quick, I . . . uh . . . didn't eat dinner yet . . ." The boy with the motorcycle mysteriously disappeared inside the house; the girls could hear him in the kitchen. It was closer to breakfast now than to dinner. Sometimes they would go eat bad eggs and burnt coffee at the local-dive-of-a-diner at 3 am, but the girls were holding out for fresh corn muffins from Giant that night. The kind that were baked fresh just for them. The kind that were so big that they needed to be eaten with two hands.

Faith sat down on his patio furniture and watched the moon make waves in the in-ground pool in the backyard. Makenzie lit a cigarette before securing an ashtray and was now looking around the back porch for something to ash in that wouldn't catch on fire.

Faith stood up, feeling that the night was slipping by them, "So what are we doing tonight?" Faith asked the boy with the goatee as if he were the planning type.

"I dunno, what do you want to do?" He looked at Faith curiously.

"Something fun. Let's just do something fun . . ." Faith shrugged, looking to the boy with the baseball hat and the boy with the mohawk for suggestions.

"Like what?" The boy with the goatee instigated.

"I dunno! Something. Let's just . . ."

And as if Faith standing up had given him an idea, the boy with the goatee swung his arms under her legs to pick her up like a baby.

"Um, okay you can carry me everywhere tonight if you want to . . ." Faith teased. She would have loved a piggyback ride or a carry everywhere they went for the rest of the night.

But the second the boy with the goatee pivoted his body towards the pool Faith knew it wasn't going to end well. She flailed and whispered a scream, "Nooooooo! No! no! no!" trying not to wake the boy with the motorcycle's parents, but maybe she should have.

Faith knew that the only place the boy with the goatee was going to carry her was going to be over the pool. And then he would let her go, but she knew he wouldn't set her down dry.

She frantically tried to twist her body free of his grasp, turning belly down like a child pretending to be superman. But his arms were made to play football and she knew that he would not fumble her. Faith turned her head back to the porch to see Makenzie putting her lit cigarette in her mouth, using her wide eyes to help press her lips hard against the filter to hold it in place as she ran fast towards Faith.

Makenzie's arms were stretched out as if Faith were falling from the sky and she had to catch her.

Faith strained her right hand, begging it to dislodge her cell phone from her back pocket. She felt the pressure of having only seconds, and she couldn't use them all to beg, that would be useless.

She had to save her phone.

She just couldn't reach it.

"Wait! My cell phone!" Faith wiggled but the boy with the goatee wasn't listening to her squirmy pleas. He had his head turned over his shoulder laughing to see the boy with the motorcycle in the doorway with a six-pack of beer in one hand and an open can in the other. Beer was his late night snack. The boy with the goatee swung Faith back around to face the porch and after seeing the boy with the motorcycle in the doorway, Faith felt saved.

All of her muscles relaxed.

She sighed.

The boy with the motorcycle wouldn't let her get thrown into the pool. He would have protected her from anything and everything, and that surely included water. He would have punched anyone right in the face who even tried to hurt her. The boy with the motorcycle was the one who brought Faith's favorite ice cream to her doorstep when she was sick at home. He was the one who woke her up after midnight in the coldest air, to make sure that she saw the start of the snow and to take her out for a drive in it. And he was the one who gave her his hoodie so that they could stay out in the cold and play just a little bit longer.

He always kept her warm.

The boy with the motorcycle wouldn't let her get thrown into the midnight-cold pool.

But he smiled.

And he nodded his head at the boy with the goatee.

It was all the encouragement the boy holding Faith needed and he quickly swung her, winding her up to let her go over the water. Faith's heart dropped. Once freed into the air her right arm quickly reached for her back pocket and pulled her cell phone out. Faith's right arm tried pushing her cell phone away from her body in the air and willing it in the direction that Makenzie was standing, but as her body was hurled to the center of the pool, her cell phone was only tossed feet from her flying body, splash-landing in the pool next to her.

Faith went under the water.

The hot summer air faded around her into cold bubbles.

And as Faith opened her eyes underwater she could see her cell phone, underwater too, staring back at her but no longer glowing. She reached out for it, and came up for air.

Everyone was laughing, except Makenzie; at least Makenzie made an attempt at pity but Faith could tell that she wanted to laugh too. Faith sighed holding her wet cell phone out of the water hoping that rice trick was true and that rice would be the hero and draw all of the moisture out of her phone. She never imagined her night would end in a broken curfew to buy rice.

Faith scowled at the boy with the goatee, wishing that she could have had the strength to pull him into the water with her.

"Hey you said something fun, swimming is always fun!" The boy with the goatee said jovially in his defense.

"Not with clothes on and your cell phone in your hand!" Faith whispered a scold in his direction while she kicked flip-flops underwater like flippers moving her to the edge of the pool. Water poured from her like a human poolside waterfall as she pulled herself up and out of the pool. She looked up at the boy with the goatee and made a face. She tried being mad at him, but she couldn't. She couldn't ever stay mad at him because he was like a brother to her. But that's what she got when he teased her like a sister.

"Geeze . . . why didn't you throw Makenzie in?!" Faith waddled with whines and wet clothes over to the patio, her shorts and T-shirt now heavy with water.

"Hey!" Makenzie laughed, and so did the other boys.

"Because she was smoking a cigarette, I didn't want to get burnt!" The boy with the goatee laughed and Makenzie took a puff of her cigarette, causing the end to glow orange, and shrugged her shoulders while nodding her head.

"Ugh . . . now I've got to be cold and wet all night." Faith made a frowning face and was hoping the boy with the motorcycle would just run into his house already and get her a towel and one of his T-shirts to wear.

"It's okay, Fay, just take off your shorts and your T-shirt and lay them out here, they will dry."

Makenzie asked her to undress nonchalantly as if wet clothes were worse that being half naked in front of people. "Um. No." Faith shook her head, looking at Makenzie with an odd look to remind her that they weren't in their bedroom at their Grandma's house putting on pjs for the night, that they were instead in the company of four boys in the middle of a large neighborhood of backyards.

"C'mon." Makenzie teased her and put out her cigarette into her makeshift ashtray of an old soda can.

"I'm not sitting here half naked all night!" Faith couldn't believe what Makenzie was really asking her to do. Like this kind of reverse baptism was necessary.

Makenzie flicked off her flip-flops and took her shirt off in one swoop of her arms over her head. She smiled at Faith, "C'mon, we'll just go swimming till your clothes dry!" And before Faith even had time to worry if her own underwear and her bra matched, Makenzie had already un-hooked and slid off her bra and was now holding her arms across her chest tip-toing-a-fairy-like-skipping-run around the outside of the pool. Before anyone even knew what was happening, Makenzie's bare legs swished through the water of the pool steps and she was up to her naked shoulders surrounded by water with a moonlit smile.

Makenzie giggled at herself, swinging her naked arms back and forth underwater.

The boys stood around the pool for only a moment of confusion before they all took Makenzie's silent but obvious dare to get into the pool too, naked.

Faith knew there was no reeling this situation back in and suddenly she felt overly attached to her cold, heavy, dripping wet clothes.

The boy with the motorcycle set down his beer and undressed, cannonballing into his pool. The boy with the mohawk and the boy with the baseball hat followed, while Makenzie laughed excitedly and clapped at the surface of the water as her crazy idea unfolded.

The boy with the goatee conceded to undress, although he didn't imagine a consequence to throwing Faith in the pool would ever be to get wet himself, or to get naked.

Faith sighed, while everyone in the pool giggled, including the boys.

Thinking about being stark naked in front of the boys gave Faith the exact same amount of panic that she had flying through the air over the pool just moments ago.

And the water-death of her cell phone was now the least of her worries.

Dripping wet, Faith went over to the porch and grabbed the six-pack of beer. She carried it beside the pool and sat down opening one for herself. She pushed out a sigh, breathing back in the smell of chlorine on her, and chugged the beer in her hand until her eyes started to water from the rush of carbonation. Everyone already in the pool just stared at her, waiting for her.

"C'mon!" Makenzie called for her, "Fay . . . you only live once!" Makenzie was whispering loud enough to make sure Faith could hear her without waking up the sleeping neighborhood. Faith knew Makenzie well enough to know the strength it was taking for her to whisper across the pool right now and not break out in the chorus of a rap song about getting naked.

"YOLO!" Everyone in the pool was now whispering to Faith. But Faith hated that worn-out anthem. It was so stupid, really. Because Faith already knew that "you only live once"; she knew that more than they did. And she knew that sometimes the "once" that she might live could be half as short as someone else's once. . . . That they should have been saying sometimes-you-only-live-half-a-once.

And only because Faith knew that her "once" could be a "half," did she undress in front of everyone staring at her, tossing her wet, limp, clothes to the arm of a poolside chair to dry.

And she jumped into the pool.

Naked.

The important memories will never leave you.
And once someone passes, they all become important.

The more time goes on, the harder it might get to share them.
Over time the details may become lost.
But you'll never forget the feelings.
        You'll never forget them.
                Never.

Because all of these memories, each smile, tear, and experience have
been woven into the exact fiber of the being that you are. You will
carry them with you in every ounce of your life.

        And you don't have to worry about forgetting them.
        Or about them forgetting you.

        Heaven could never forget you.

. . . .

Back at the house that isn't mine I feel more prepared in the only way that I can feel prepared now, I have an outfit for the fourth worst day of my life—even though I will feel completely bare to the skin naked and vulnerable in front of hundreds of people tomorrow.

And deep down I already know that for the rest of my life I will be trying to cover up from the feeling of being naked.

Death strips everyone bare.

I carry in shoeboxes of pictures to the house and I'm glad to see people there, waiting for me, with construction paper, poster board, and frames. I scatter everything and I start trying to cut printed copies of pictures, but my fingers can't work the scissors. My sadness is crippling.

I get frustrated and shake thoughts from my head. All this is about to break me, all over again. These damn scissors will be what breaks me.

And then a voice asks from beyond the fog that death created, "What can I do to help?" and it's the girl with the soft voice, patient and gentle, sitting beside me waiting for whatever I say next. She's the friend who doesn't need words. She's the friend who can sit next to me in silence and we can still have a complete conversation. And I'm glad to have her next to me now. I hand her the scissors and point to pictures that need trimmed in order fit into frames.

And we sit, making memories into mini-memorials.

The girl with the soft voice holds up a picture and asks, "When was this one taken . . . ?" And she holds the picture carefully by the edges, she knows that these pictures are all that I have left, and even they tell a lie. I think about my cousin and me in the "selfie" that my friend is now holding, and how neither one of us will ever be those two same people again. She got promoted to angel wings. And I have to walk the Earth to feel all the pain of a rapture gone wrong. "Just last summer . . ." I say.

"It's a nice picture, do you want to use this one?" her voice is gentle and safe and so I tell her the secret behind the girls' sparkling eyes in the photo.

"No . . . we were crying our eyes out right before the picture was taken. We were at an ice cream stand and neither of us wanted ice cream. It was one of the times that I had to leave her, but I don't know why that one really hurt the most. It's like we both knew. We just couldn't stop crying over that damn ice cream." I tell her proudly, "But when we were crying I told her I was going to take a picture of us so we'd remember that it wasn't always going to be that bad, and she laughed thinking about us having a picture of us crying and how freaking weird that would be." The girl with the soft voice's face agreed that she'd never seen a picture of two grown girls crying with ice cream before. And I let something out that sounded like my voice reaching to laugh again, "She didn't want an ugly-cry picture. So we just tried to laugh."

And of all the pictures reminding me of the past it's the only one here giving me any kind of clue to the future. She would remind me that we just have to smile through the tears. She'd be endlessly repeating those words into my face if she were here. And I wish she were here right now more than I wish we would have just ordered more ice cream that day.

I dig through another box of stacked memories and a folded note on ruled paper pops up between photos and cards. Even from the backside of the twice folded note I can tell that it's her handwriting on the inside, and it feels like a present to unwrap. My hands start to shake. They tremble at the gentle force needed to carefully open the letter without ripping it at the folds, full of excitement to read it. I unfold and flatten the note and even though I remember that it was she who gave this to me, right now I feel like it's a gift from God. Suddenly everything she ever gave to anyone is a gift from God, and now everyone realizes that she was the gift.

She was always a gift.

I read the note and remember exactly what day it's from and although I've read it before it feels like I'm reading it for the first time. I take in the way she loops her g's and how happy and alive her r's look. Each word looks like it's bouncing off the paper. And then my eyes catch a sentence in the two pages of text that takes me both back in time and into the present:

". . . *You know what, life's just CRAZY. It's one wild ride, like a roller coaster it has its scary turns and ups and downs, but there's nothing we can do about it. We just have to hold on tight. And most importantly, you have to stay on the ride. We just can't get off the ride. Even if I'm not always sitting next to you.*

Even if we are far apart, I'll always have your back, like a guardian angel, but without the wings . . ."

I've read this letter before.
But reading it now is different.
Because I know she's really an angel now.
    And because she knew.
        She always knew.

Makenzie

Chain eating mints should have reminded her of summers in her Grandpa's garden when she was little and pulling leaves off mint bushes to run away just to return to chew more, like a mint-eating-butterfly, but instead the taste of mints only reminded her of the vile smell of bile that her mouth was constantly bringing up.

She popped a mint in her mouth and tried not to think about vomiting.

"I'm tired, Fay." Makenzie looked out the passenger window at the streets that were leading her home and she wished instead that they could just keep driving all night like they did on the weekends.

"Yeah, I'm pretty tired too." Just talking about being tired made Faith's eyes yawn as she opened them wide from behind the steering wheel.

"No, Fay. I'm *tired*. I don't want to go home . . ."

"What do you mean?" Faith turned her head quickly towards Makenzie before looking back out at the road again.

"This place, is beating me down Fay, this house and everything in it, I feel like I'm suffocating the closer we get to it. I just. I can't even breathe there anymore without being yelled at. I can't do anything right and it's like every day is so clear to me that they don't want me there."

"It'll be alright Mazie . . ."

"No Faith. It won't. . . . When you close your eyes, what color do you see?" Makenzie sat up and turned towards the center of the car.

"Oh . . . I dunno . . . I guess, I think . . . maybe I dream in color? Why, what do you dream in, gray? Does that mean something?" Faith looked like she had never thought about it before. Makenzie thought about it all the time.

"That's the difference between us, Fay." Makenzie had an I-told-you-so tone in her voice, "I used to see in color when I was awake and dreaming, and now I Just see gray when I open my eyes. . . . And it makes me not want to see anything anymore . . . I'm so tired of it all. I'm so tired of feeling this way. Of not feeling good enough, of feeling wrong, of feeling stupid. . . . I just don't want to feel anything anymore." Makenzie looked back out the passenger window as if it were Faith she were mad at just then and not her life.

"Makenzie . . ." Faith said her name but it sounded like "C'mon" or "knock it off."

Makenzie just stared out the window wishing for things.

Without a response Faith sped up.

"What are you doing, Fay?!" The last thing Makenzie wanted was to get home any faster than they already were driving. Makenzie watched two stop signs go by the side of her window like flashes of red. "Fay! STOP! That means Stop!"

"What? You don't want to be here, right? Isn't that what you just said?" Faith drove fearlessly.

"That's not what I mean, Fay!"

"Yeah, it is!" Faith looked at Makenzie instead of the road.

"Fay, slow down!" and almost as soon as Makenzie said it Faith slammed on the brakes. They were in the middle of an intersection. At night. And Faith switched off the headlights.

The car was silent for only a moment before Makenzie retracted her plea from a second ago, now asking, "Faith, please go!"

Makenzie looked at Faith with sorry eyes for ever saying she wanted to give up, but the look alone wasn't enough now.

"No. You don't want to be here, what's the difference if I'm not here either." Faith shrugged her shoulders and pretended to look comfortable.

"Because this isn't about you, I don't want you to die because I feel this way, you don't get it . . ."

They sat.

And the car was silent for just long enough before Faith's hands erupted off the wheel and she shouted,

"No, you don't get it. I know how you feel, Makenzie, everybody feels that way sometimes, okay? And I know how you throw up when you're alone, I fucking know. And don't think for one second that when you hurt yourself that it doesn't fucking hurt me. It hurts everyone who's ever loved you. So knock it off! Life isn't supposed to make you feel good, or make you feel bad, life is just supposed to make you feel . . . okay? Somewhere along the line people get to thinking that life is supposed to always be perfect and feel so fucking great all the time, well most of the time it doesn't. It's not the Disney fairytale we believed it was when we were six, being a teenager is hard. It just sucks. And the other part of the time, when it doesn't suck, we don't even notice. That's life, so sometimes it is gray but it's not always going to be . . . it's not going to be gray forever . . ."

Somewhere in Faith's rant Makenzie started to cry and now she had slow solid tears running down both cheeks. She never wanted Faith to hurt and she never wanted to be the one to hurt her. With an honest look, Makenzie turned to Faith and said "I'm sorry."

The car was silent for just another second before Makenzie heard the car kick back into gear.

"Good." Faith said as she turned her headlights back on and the street in front of them was revealed again.

And as if the two of them weren't just shouting tears at each other moments earlier, Makenzie said calmly, "That was really good Fay, that thing about life not being good or bad but just being. I needed to hear that." Makenzie had had a million thoughts running rapidly through her brain for days, but now there was just that one. And it felt really good.

"Thanks, but I can't take the credit, I think it's a quote from somewhere." Faith admitted part of her genius may have been plagiarized.

"Well, thanks." Makenzie wiped another tear but she was smiling again.

"Hey, we're done crying now," Faith joked.

"I know! But I can't stop though!" Makenzie laughed through snot and laughed at the amount of tears she didn't know she had been holding back. Now that she let one out, she couldn't shut them off. "Fay, I promise I won't be stupid anymore. I won't think like that. I don't want to be like this."

"I know, Mazie." Faith let out a deep sigh, "It's not always going to be this way. I promise."

And that was all Makenzie needed to hear, to believe that things would start to get better.

Because Faith knew.

She always knew.

Death will drive you mad.

You won't know what you're doing.
        Who you are.
                Or who you used to be.

Death will put parts of you on autopilot
        And other parts will get shut down completely.
        And whatever's left, will never be the same again.

The rest of your life will be spent trying to get back to
        "normal."
                But "normal" doesn't exist.
                It never did.

. . . .

I sit on the floor of the living room of the house that isn't mine, closest to the ground and closest to the door—the door that is never locked.

I can see the colors of the night through the window in the front door from where I sit. And I know now that I have collected another sunset without her and now face the burden of surviving another night ahead of me.

I wonder if I will always feel like running away or if one day I might be able to sit comfortably on a chair in a room of people and not have it sting. Maybe one day I'll be able to sink into a couch with a sigh instead of feeling suffocated. Maybe one day I'll even be able to sleep in a bed again without fear. Maybe. I dunno. But that day isn't today.

I sit on the hard floor, legs crossed, hunched over.
There's safeness in the discomfort now.
Safeness in being as low to the ground as possible.
No phone call can ever break me to the ground if I am already here.

Someone hands me another beer and I concede. I don't really want to drink at all. There's nothing to celebrate, but they say, "Let's make a cheers! To her!" and I nod my head in a shrug as they turn their long neck bottles askew and reach over to clank mine. The sound lingers for a moment, we take a sip, and it's over.

The alcohol numbs me in perfect timing. Silent thoughts and feelings start to rise up like the tiny bubbles of carbonation trapped inside the beer in my hand and I'm too weak to fight them. Eighteen is too young to drink alcohol, I know that, and not just legally—emotionally. Eighteen has too much pain. And we're all trying to put out these fires within us with ice cold beers, but one after another is proving no help at all. Being young is volatile. But then again, so is being an adult, as I'm finding out.

I take a sip.
And another.

The friends in the room move on to other conversations and I try to listen but I can't process what they're saying. I can't understand the words and phrases and feelings of their stories that have nothing to do with her. I sit, feeling even more confused.
My heart beats rapidly.
And I take another sip.

Someone asks me what I think about something and I can't say anything . . . about *anything*. I shrug. I have no opinions. I have no voice. They move on with their stories and every conversation is foreign to me because these conversations, like me—are all just missing her.
And I take another sip, focusing on the lack of her in everything around me. The fact that it's possible for them to talk and to even think about anything other than her right now is almost more painful than losing her. It's like losing her all over again in a way I didn't think I'd have to worry about. I didn't think there was anything else to prepare for, and I'm left not only alone sitting on the cold floor, but feeling stupid. I thought losing her was final, I didn't realize that I'd have to lose her again in so many ways. I have a sinking feeling in my stomach.
Death is internal quicksand.
I listen as hard as I can to their conversations and try to be where they are.
But I'm not.
I'm as far away from them as I can be for someone sitting so close. I wish I could talk about meaningless things like they are right now, but I can't do it.
I just can't.
Something in my stomach feels like failure as I think about how I couldn't even deposit my paycheck at the bank today because even though I rehearsed the words in my head a hundred times while waiting in line, somehow I couldn't say "*I would like to deposit this into my checking please.*" I don't know if it was the red roped cattle shoot waiting for the next teller or because those words would have been the first arrangement of sounds that I said that had nothing to do with her, but I couldn't do it.

I think about how stupid it is.

How can words that have nothing to do with her be so hard to say? You would think that they would be the easiest to say. I should have no problem saying things that have no attachment to anything. You would think that words free from feelings and emotions should be the only things I can find to say for the rest of my life, but it feels like the opposite.

It doesn't make any sense.

This life makes no sense.

And I take another sip.

And I think about ducking under the red velvet rope today and covering my mouth as I briskly walked out of the bank with check in hand. I think about how I can feel the folds of the check still in my back pocket that I'm sitting on now.

I take another sip.

Someone comes over and hands me another beer and I realize that the one I'm holding is now empty. Everyone here in the house that isn't mine is looking out for me in different ways. Some think that this beer is what I need now. But I don't think any of them really know what I need. Not what I need most.

I am just half dead now, visiting with the living, and they are all just trying to be good hosts, and take care of me. And bring me things, like more drinks.

Music is playing in the living room and it's loud, I think, but I could be in a room in complete silence all by myself and think it were too loud right now. Everything is just too much. I try to listen to the music, it's familiar, and I know it is, but I can't find the same feelings that I used to feel when I'd hear this same song. This song used to make me feel like summer even in the dead of winter, and now it's an opposite I never imagined: it's the middle of summer and this song is just making me feel all of the death.

In my mind I'm drowning out the lyrics to only hear the music, and once I do I can hear something else. A faint steady beat of rain coming down on the roof and bouncing off the windows and I feel . . . anxious.

I walk over and open the screen door. I slide out slowly and the music is just loud enough to cover up the "click" of the metal handle catching behind me.

As soon as I step on to the porch, splashes of rain come find me standing under the small overhang of the roof and I do not refuse the invitation. I set down the bottle I'm holding and I walk out into the driveway and stand, looking up into the dark sky, watching the drops come down over everything. The street, houses, cars, trees are all lit with the golden wet reflection from streetlights. I wonder if I too have this halo-type glow around me from the reflection of streetlights in the rain.

And I think about how this might be the glow that Heaven has.

Except without the cold, wet feeling.

And then I realize as the dark blues and blacks of the empty night flood my eyes . . . that this is nothing like Heaven. Whatever my eyes see from now on will forever be the opposite of Heaven. But for the first time, in three days, I can feel something other than empty, I can feel the rain now. I can feel every single drop pricking me, poking at me, and sliding down my face to stroke my body.

It seems like I've never felt the rain like this before, welcoming it so much.

And if she were here, I would be sitting in the rain with her and I would tell her how the rain has never felt truer than it does now.

And if she were here, she would already know.

I try to look up at the sky, but it's too messy and I'm too far away to see our star. And it's the smallest things, like missing "our star" that break me down again and again, as I start to cry in the rain now. I fold in half on the soaking shiny pavement and my elbows rest on my knees bringing my open palms to my face. The only relief I have is that there's something about the rain that doesn't make the endless tears hurt as bad. Maybe it's the cold numbing my face, or maybe it's the water washing off the sting of fresh tears before the salt in them has a chance to burn, but the pouring rain makes the tears more welcome. I lean back and look at the cloudy blackness that is the night sky and I can see big drops coming down. I let them fall on to my face and with my head leaning back I close my eyes.

I'm sitting in the rain, appreciating every drop, but I just wish that I could feel her here too. I can't stop wishing that she were sitting in the rain beside me. But she's not. And I'm alone. And I just want to feel as alone as I really am, and let the loneliness shower over me. I just want to be accustomed to this pain already so that I will become numb to it like the alcohol has numbed my senses.

Rain is the only sound that even when loudly pounding, can feel like a warm blanket of silence.

Then I hear the music again, funneling out to me. Someone has opened the front door and is calling to me from the dryness of the porch. They are calling, surprised that I'm outside, and I say "I'm fine."

They yell again, they seem panicked. Yelling, because I'm soaking wet in the rain, alone.

I yell over the rain that "I'm fine," "I know," and "it's okay."

I am a million things right now, but I guess being wet upsets them the most. They have concern on their face and they yell back in the house over their shoulder, still watching me like I am a small child, while they call for the boys to come get me. I don't want to go back inside though. I can't go back in yet. I felt more alone inside with those people than I did out here in the rain. The more people in front of me that aren't her, the more I need her.

And I know that they don't get it.

The rest of my life is going to be pouring rain.

They need to give me a chance, they need to let me just stand in it. How else will I ever get used to this monsoon season in my life if they don't let me be submersed in it now.

And now the boy with the goatee and the boy with the motorcycle are on the porch and looking around for me. They both take long strides as if to try and dodge the large raindrops, on their way to retrieve me. The boy with the mohawk follows them out once he sees what's going on, but I stand up and I shake my head back and forth and I back away from them all as they come closer.

"I'm fine!" I shake my head and I even try to smile, to convince them to let me stay.

The boy with the goatee says, "C'mon, let's go back inside," his voice forceful but his arms reach for me gently. And I trust him like a brother, but not in this moment. I don't want to go back inside now.

"I don't want to!" If I could explain it to them in a way that they would understand I would, but the look in their eyes say they don't have time for explanations. The boy with the motorcycle's shoulders are hunched tense from the falling rain. He is reaching for me and his arms are begging me to trust him as if I'm standing on the outside ledge of an office building and he's coaxing me back through an open window telling me not to jump. The boy with the mohawk looks tired and so does his hair as it's getting more wet the longer he's outside.

They're all trying to help me.

But they're all looking at me like I'm wrong.

I'm not wrong.

Everything else is wrong.

And they don't get it.

They just don't get it.

But I know that she would. She would understand. She would have come out here and taken my hand and sat with me in the rain until I felt like it was okay to go on, and then we would have jumped in the puddles, at least one, to show this world who was boss, before we went back inside to dry off. And then we'd have hot chocolate.

I can't believe we'll never have hot chocolate again.

And now, in the middle of July I'm soaking wet and crying over hot chocolate. That's the way death fucking goes. I will always have the pain of wanting something that I can't have.

But these guys, they don't understand why I need to be out here. And it's making it obvious to me now, that I am completely alone, in this feeling and in this world. They're pulling at my arms to bring me in, like a criminal. But I'm not on a ledge and I'm not crazy. I resist again and shout at them over the rain, "I'm fine! You don't need to be outside! I'm fine!" I look at the boy with the mohawk and plead with my eyes to just go back inside and leave me here.

"We're not going back inside without you!" The boy with the goatee is already dripping wet. His slippery hands touch my shoulders loosely. And I believe him. I know they won't go back inside without me and I both love them and hate them all for that right now, and for a moment I feel like conceding to defeat. One of the boys comes up behind me, hugging me from behind like he's done a hundred times before. He holds my wrists and folds them across my chest into me, and he squeezes. He just wants to let me know that he's here for me and that I'm safe in his arms, but as he folds my limp wet arms across my chest underneath his, trying to comfort me, I can't separate myself from the feeling of her dead arms folded across her chest somewhere right now.

The pain of that image fills me.

And right now, putting me back into that house feels the same as when I think about them putting her into that coffin.

And I can't do it.

I can't let them box me up and I can't let them do the same to her. And I swing my arms loose, to free myself.

And I swing them again, hard, for her.

And I run.

My legs pound at the street like the rain, and I feel like I could run forever. I have no plan other than to run. I just want to stay in the rain until it stops, until all of this just stops.

I just need to know that it will stop.

It has to.

The boys mumble at each other and I can hear them start to run after me. I know they are mad. I start to cry again. I'm not crazy, but they think I am. And I realize this is how the rest of my life might very well feel like.

Being chased, in the rain, on a sad empty night, without a plan.

And for the first time I realize that my life previous to this actually did have a plan. It wasn't great. But it was an idea of how things were going to be, maybe not long term, but day to day at least. And for the first time, it feels like if I lived that awful crazy mixed-up life with a mild plan for just a minute again that I would be okay.

The heaviness of the rest of my life lands hard on my shoulders with every thought and every drop of falling rain.

And then I see it.

I see a truck.

Shiny from the rain it looks brand new.

Its bed is empty.

I slow my feet and I run my hand along the back of a stranger's truck from five houses up. It feels like if I just climb into the back of this truck that I can go back in time. Even for just a moment, and I can feel okay again for just a second. I just need to feel okay. I need to touch at least one memory, and so I climb in and I lay down. The truck bed is hard and the rain is gentle. I think about all the nights we spent in the back of a light blue beat up truck bed looking at the stars, and I just want to feel that way again.

I hear the boys getting closer, the pounding of their feet quickens and I can hear them shuffle as they see me lying down. I knew they would catch up to me, I knew they would find me, but I just wish they would climb into the back of this stranger's truck with me, at midnight, and pretend like everything was okay again. Just for a minute.

I feel so desperate for one minute, like it's all that I might need to get me through one more day.

But they can't. They can't pretend that everything is okay because it will never be okay again.

We will never be okay again.

I look up at the rain as it falls down, each drop taking a lifetime to get to me. Everything feels like slow motion.

They quietly unlatch the strangers tailgate and fold it down.

And I can feel two sets of hands wrap around my ankles and hold tight.

Their hands are slippery from the rain but I know that they won't let me go again, I know the chase is over. And I know that I can't just jump into an old memory.

But I had to try.

And on my belly now, drenched in sadness, they slowly pull me out of the empty truck bed by my bare feet. The ribs of the bed are parallel to my outstretched body and I think about all the times the hard plastic from one of these beds left her with bruises on her summer legs after taking late night joy rides, riding in the back illegally touring our sleepy town at 2 am and seeing it in a way no one else would appreciate it. We always bruised so easily from the bumps and turns throwing us from side to side.

And now, death is a bruise that will last forever.

My hands are stretched out, reaching for something, anything to hold on to. I can only grab at the grooves in the truck bed as I'm being pulled out. But my fingers are defeated too, only slipping into the tiny pools of water collected in the small ridges of plastic.

There's nothing left to grab on to.

Everything's over.

And I can't hold on to any of it anymore.

The boys pick me up and set me on my feet. And with one on each side of me and one behind me to make sure I don't make another attempt to run, they walk me back to the house that isn't mine.

They don't say anything, but I can feel what they are thinking.

Something about the rain makes me feel everything so much more.

The sidewalk in front of me feels like it will never end.

And even though I know where it's leading and I know exactly where we are going,

I've never felt so lost.

Faith

She was having a flare-up. She hated the term, "flare-up." It's what all the doctors called it when things were *happening*. The cutting abdominal pain. The diarrhea. The fatigue. The fever. The bleeding. When she was doing everything that they told her to do and taking every awful medication possible, the bleeding still came back.

Still.

"It's just a flare-up," they said. The phrase itself didn't reveal anything about the seriousness of the situation. It sounded like she was just lighting sparklers or something; having a flare-up made it sound like the opposite of dying. But what was happening wasn't short blasts of starry fireworks flaring up with hissing sparks that only lasted two minutes. A flare up could last a year.

365 days.

Over 31 million seconds of bleeding.

They should have called it a bleed out.

Bleeding that consistently was just not normal. Even girls on their period have at least one moment every month where they feel like bleeding for five days straight is just not okay. It's gross. And it's depressing. To see blood. To smell it. To have to wipe away at your own stain, look at it, and know that it came out of you.

To look at how disgusting you actually are and to hold the truth of your sickening filth, for just a moment, in your own hands.

She was lying in a hospital gown with a green and brown square print—depending on the angle, if she turned her head, diamonds. The gown looked awful but was less baggy on her than half of her clothes now were. She was hooked up to a machine, that beeped loudly out from her room into the hallway of the Hospital and she could hear other machines beeping back at her from several doors down. Like a constant marco-polo of dogs in a neighborhood howling and barking in the middle of the night at nothing, those stupid machines just wouldn't stop echoing each other.

A Doctor walked in with a clipboard sooner than any other white-lab-coat-wearing-person she had ever seen before, and she had seen a lot; they always made her wait. Faith and her mom had waited days before, weeks even for tests while they kept her in the Hospital, and this one had come back in minutes.

Just minutes.

He didn't even give them time to wonder,

or worry,

or pray.

Faith didn't even have time to guess if she might trust what he was going to say. She looked at the Doctor standing in the doorway and wished for just a second that they could be friends, or neighbors, or maybe that she could even know his first name. Whatever he was going to say next, she just didn't want him to be a stranger.

"Don't say it like a stranger," she hoped in her head as he walked quickly to her, *"Please don't say it like a stranger . . ."*

Faith knew it was going to be bad news, and that it would hurt so much worse if bad news came from a stranger.

Faith looked at her mom.

She looked back at the Doctor.

And she braced for impact.

Makenzie

She wanted to cry.

But she didn't.

She only pleaded with Faith as if Faith had any final say in the matter. As if any of us really decide our own fate.

"You can't die, Fay. You're not going to, okay. You're going to die long after me." Her words felt like a wish as they came out, like she wasn't sure. Makenzie gave a beggar's smile to Faith.

"Makenzie, I'm going to die before you. Okay, that's just the way it is. I'm sick, and you're not. And no matter what I'm always going to be sick. And the more time that goes on, the sicker I will get. That's a fact, those are the odds." Faith shrugged her shoulders.

More than anything about the conversation itself, Makenzie hated Faith's tone of voice when they talked about her being sick. She hated how calm Faith was. How could she just be so matter of a fact with this all?

It wasn't normal.

And it wasn't okay.

"No, Fay. You have to die after me, c'mon just say it—you know I wouldn't last a day without you. You know I couldn't. My life would be so royally fucked up if you weren't here to save me. I'm not as strong as you. I can't be like you—I can't be just okay with this." Makenzie made the most serious face that her personality would let her make.

"Makenzie, I'm not going to agree to that, okay. It's just silly. You're stronger than you think, you're a stronger person than me. You can handle anything."

"No I can't, Fay! Not without you! We could be 88 years old in a nursing home and I swear to God if you died before me I would pull my own plug! I swear!" Makenzie raised her eyebrows and nodded her head quickly with tears in her eyes.

"Mazie . . ." Faith sighed at trying to find a happy medium, "If we live to be 88, I promise you can die first."

"Okay, good! Thank you!" Makenzie couldn't believe that she had just won that argument and pushed the envelope a little further, "Can I also have the bed that faces the window side of the nursing home room that we will share . . . ?"

"Sure . . ." Faith smiled like she meant it.

Faith

She didn't know why but everything was harder than it had to be. It was 6 am and already it was hard for her to walk. Yesterday was okay, and tomorrow might be better, but today was proving to be hard. And that's just the way it went.

Getting out of bed to go to the bathroom, she held her stomach and tried to remember if she took her pills on time the night before. With the morning fog she couldn't recall much, but it didn't matter. It was all trivial because those pills she took weren't magic beans. They couldn't grow her a new intestinal lining or immune system. They only masked the symptoms just enough. They would never erase the disease.

The disease was incurable.

Days like this were simply reminders of that.

She held her stomach with one hand and her head with the other as she limped and got as far as her dresser by her bedroom doorway before she was knocking things over and breathing in only pain. It started in her stomach and in the last four steps she had taken it had echoed through her whole body.

Her arms got tense and her legs weakened.

She held both hands on her dresser.

The pain snowballed inside her.

She could see the hallway and the bathroom through the crack of her bedroom door, but she couldn't move. She could only hold on to the dresser tighter. Tears started to fill her eyes and she blinked them away. She couldn't be defeated this early. She gripped the dresser at her waist level with one hand and forced the other around her stomach.

She held her breath.

She told herself that she was fine.

It' okay.

This will end.

And then she reminded herself that she never wanted this.

With another pulse of pain through her body followed by chills, she opened her eyes. It was over in probably a minute's time, but to her it felt like a never-ending nightmare. She stood without the dresser's help and fixed the things she had knocked down in her earthquake of pain. She sat back upright a bottle of perfume, a picture frame, and a little figurine. Faith looked at her dresser and wondered how she would get though the day. How could she walk through halls at school and climb sets of stairs to classes if she couldn't even walk four feet to the bathroom without using the wall and her dresser to hold her upright. She wasn't going to make it.

She was never going to make much of anything.

Not with this disease.

Then, while still steadying herself with one hand, she saw the three large containers of pills in the center of her dresser.

Her invisible crutches.

Her added symptoms.

The ugly non-curers of disease.

Towering over everything, the prescription bottles stood tall with warning labels stickered up and down them. Suggestions of when to take the pills and what to take them with. Little stupid rules on top of other stupid rules for a game that she never wanted to play.

Those stupid pills. They didn't stop any of this. They just let her fall. And with the strength she didn't have just a minute ago she took her right hand and she swung it, backhanding all of the pill bottles at once.

The tall pill cylinders clanked together, shaking like maracas to the floor.

The
Goodbye

You can spend your whole life trying to say goodbye to one person.
Goodbyes are never easy.

The word itself carries eons of pains from a million
heartbreaks. Heartbreaks from around the world that you know
nothing about, but yet you can somehow feel their pain coming along
with yours like they're waves in the ocean of your goodbye.

Even if their last breath would have stretched out to a week, you
wouldn't have ever said goodbye.
You wouldn't have used that word.
Because it's not Goodbye.

Goodbyes are only for people you never want to see again—people
you want to hurt just by saying a word filled with pain. You would
have never said a word like that.

Because you will see them again.
Heaven knows you will.

. . . .

The planning is mostly done.
And now, we just procrastinate life while waiting for the funeral.

      The weight of tomorrow is seeping into today, and all I can think about is how I don't want to say goodbye to her. But now there is this thing, this big event created to do just that, for everyone to say goodbye.
      And I don't want to do it.
      But I have to.
      I have to be there, be present in the middle of all of this pain. I have to greet people and hug them on her behalf. I have to play hostess to this hell. And more importantly, I have to be there to remind people that she lived. I have to tell them how much she loved them all.

      But I don't need to spill out my love for her in a tear-choked confession of a goodbye. I have no guilt. I have no ungiven hugs. I have no regrets. And for that reason, and that reason only, I will be the strongest person in that funeral room tomorrow. Because I told her how much I loved her every chance I got.
      She knew.
         She will always know.

Makenzie

She didn't expect a week ago that she'd be crying over lumpy mashed potatoes at Cracker Barrel, but goodbyes always made her cry. The plan to move from her dad's to her mom's had all happened too fast. One day she felt unwelcomed at her dad and stepmom's house and the next day she really was. She didn't know what to do, where to go, but she knew that she couldn't live in that house anymore. Because the only thing worse than not knowing where she belonged was knowing where she didn't.

She was too full with the feeling of being unwanted to eat anything now, but she just wanted to sit with Faith, at a restaurant. Maybe if they were out in public, they wouldn't cry so much. And maybe if it was at a restaurant it could feel more like a celebration of things to come. It took Makenzie all but promising not to move a whole state away for Faith to agree to go out to dinner with her that day but it had been silence since they sat down.

"So, what's great is that my mom sounded really excited for me to move there, she said that we could go shopping for a dresser at Ikea as soon as I get there . . ." Makenzie moved the gravy pile from on top of her chicken with the back of her fork over to her potatoes and tried thinking about how eventually everything has to move. Everyone has to move on in time. She was just moving first. And moving at this time in her life, would make the rest of her life easier.

"And she was telling me about all the great colleges in Maryland, and there's a community college right by my mom's house so after senior year she said I can go there. I can go to college, Fay!" Makenzie was excited at the prospect of college, something her dad always told her she didn't need. Having a sure way to go to college was so exciting to her that starting over somewhere new before her junior year would be worth it.

"That's great, Makenzie." Faith sighed and picked up the salt and pepper shakers at the table and shook them back and forth over her meatloaf until the square piece of meat looked like it was breaded in seasoning.

"And she said you can come down whenever you want to visit, anytime, there is an extra room." Makenzie swirled her fork around her mashed potatoes as if it were a pile of spaghetti. And she watched the gravy swirl into the milky white potatoes until the white of the potatoes and the brown of the gravy mixed completely together like paint to form a beige blob.

"Of. Course. I'll. Visit." Faith pushed around macaroni and cheese on her plate and set her fork down without even trying to take a bite of comfort food. Makenzie watched Faith reach for her purse and knew she was getting her new medicine that had to be taken with food, even though Faith hadn't taken a single bite yet.

"And she said that as soon as I get there she and my stepdad will teach me how to drive, and they have two cars so I can use one when they aren't!" Makenzie looked up from her plate at Faith, waiting for Faith's excitement to follow, "So I can come back to Pennsylvania and visit too!"

"That's great, it's all really great . . ." Faith tried sounding excited for her, but Makenzie could see that she couldn't help but shake her head as she talked. Faith threw a handful of pills back in her throat and took a sip of iced tea, keeping her eyes on the plate of meatloaf in front of her.

Makenzie knew that any amount of excitement that they both tried to conjure up for her new start was just masking the pain and the disappointment of her having to leave. Makenzie was trying so hard to list all of the "pros" about the situation without talking about, or thinking about, the one big "con." Leaving. Leaving everything, including Faith. Letting herself think of that one "con" for even just a second, gave the tears waiting on standby a green light.

The waitress came up to refill their drinks and ask if the food was okay, because neither of their plates had been touched.

"Yeah . . . we're fine . . . thanks . . ." Makenzie said while grabbing her napkin and wiping a tear. She tried to blink them away before they started coming, but the whole wooden décor of the Cracker Barrel was enough to make anyone's eyes bleed to begin with.

"Aw are you guys best friends separating for college?" the waitress asked sympathetically filling up their waters, adding, "We've had a lot of friends leaving for school, guess it's that time of year when everyone goes away to college!"

"No." Faith corrected her, "I mean, we're best friends, but she's just . . . moving." The situation would have been happier and more hopeful if they were just going to college. Makenzie wished that college was their biggest problem.

"Oh, sorry to hear that . . ." The waitress excused herself.

"But Faith, you are going to college, you know how important that is, right?" Makenzie tried to veer off the subject.

"I don't think so, Mazie. That's a whole year away, anyways. Who knows."

"You're going Fay, it's important!"

Faith let out a long sigh and stabbed her fork into the chunk of meatloaf, "Just tell me exactly when you're leaving. Okay?" Faith didn't look up at Makenzie, she just moved things around on her full plate.

Makenzie hated the accusation that she was leaving. She didn't want to think of it like that. She hated feeling like the one who was just giving up because in her mind she wasn't running away, in her mind she was just trying to gain the one thing her heart needed most in the last ten years, a Mom.

Someone to give her a hug every day. Someone who would make an extra cup of coffee or tea in the morning just for her. Someone who would worry about what she was eating during the day and who would worry what she was doing at night.

She just wished starting over could happen without feeling like she was quitting.

She wished for a lot of things.

Faith

Riding around in the boy with the goatee's jeep at midnight, Faith tried to pretend like it wasn't the last time they'd all be hanging out together. But it was. And anything they did that might be exciting or fun that night would just be them pretending. Pretending that everything was okay. Pretending that nothing would change. But everyone knew it would change.

Because the changing had already started.

Makenzie was riding shotgun instead of sitting on the shitty-hump-of-a-middle-back-seat. Makenzie unnaturally loved sitting in the middle of the back seat hump but tonight the boys made her sit up front. Tonight she was the guest of honor in their shenanigans and their time together was already slipping away.

Headed to the 24-hour car wash after taking the jeep off-roading, Makenzie turned around quickly in the front passenger seat. Her face was lit by the glow of the stereo and the passing streetlamps, the tears in her eyes reflecting the light.

"This song, right? I know it's making me sad too. Change the station already." Faith nodded her head acknowledging that she was already thinking of Makenzie being gone soon without Eagle Eye Cherry bringing it all back from the 90s.

"No," Makenzie shook her head, "Fay!"

"What?!" Faith didn't know what she did wrong, and leaned in so the boy with the motorcycle sitting beside her wouldn't hear her being scolded over the music.

"It hurts!" Makenzie's voice cracked and scared Faith.

"What does . . . leaving?" Faith leaned closer and Makenzie pointed to her throat.

"My throat hurts so bad, I'm having the worst acid reflux, I . . ."

"I don't know what to do, what can I do?!" Faith wondered if stopping at the all-night pharmacy for Pepto-Bismol would really be any kind of permanent cure to calm the stomach acid in Makenzie's gut after it had already been trained to come up so often.

"There's nothing you can do, I'm just . . ." Makenzie sounded like what she meant to say was that she was mad. Pissed. Angry maybe. She looked like she could have screamed.

But she didn't say anything. She just left Faith with a fill in the blank, but it wasn't meant to be funny like an awful-drunken-game-of "Cards Against Humanity" kind-of-blank. It was the saddest-of-real-life-kind. Where someone just stops talking because they don't want to hear what they were about to say. Faith reached up for her hand and Makenzie squeezed back with teary eyes.

Faith hoped more than anything that the word Makenzie couldn't say wasn't "regretting."

Makenzie

He didn't need to say it, but he did. And the very sentence that she dreamed the boy with the mohawk would say to her the last few weeks, started with the words, "My mom said . . ."

Those words, to a teenager, can mean everything or nothing.

This time they meant everything.

"My mom said that you can stay with us for as long as you wanted." The boy with the mohawk scooped his hands into the front pockets of his blue jeans. When it felt like no one wanted her, he offered to have her permanently.

But it wasn't that easy. Faith's mom, her grandma, and two of her friends had already said the same thing. If she just dropped out of high school there wouldn't be a problem, but she couldn't just switch schools and not live with a legal guardian. Makenzie hated being so close to an adult in age but following rules for children. Especially when it felt like those rules were breaking her.

There was no other solution. Makenzie had thought about it and played out a million scenarios in her head including panhandling, but she didn't have any street-worthy skills.

But he tried to save her.

He wanted her to stay.

It didn't matter that they were standing in the middle of the town carnival and their conversation took place in front of the spinning wheel that gave out quarters when it landed on a number, clicking a hundred times before it even started to slow down. He was placing his bet on her. He wanted her to stay.

She wished so badly that she could have said yes, she wished it more than how many people were around them pushing past to get good seats on the grassy hill for the fireworks that would start soon and mark the end of the carnival and the end of the summer.

She wished she could have said yes and left with him that night and just started over in a way that wouldn't seem so scary . . .
The carnival air smelled like a funnel cake and all she wanted was a cigarette.

"Hey we're going to go find seats for the fireworks!" Faith and the girl with the dimples hopped by people standing in front of the carnival tents, waving and motioning to Makenzie where they would be. Makenzie nodded, but she didn't want to move. She just wanted to stand there, with him, forever.

The boy with the mohawk was still standing close enough to her to see every one of her eyelashes, and he raised his hand to her face with his thumb out. He gently pressed his thumb to her cheekbone where a loose eyelash had fallen.

The eyelash was now on his thumb.

And she raised her thumb to meet his, squeezing the eyelash.

Their two thumbs, held in the air against each other, made the shape of a wishbone.

"Make a wish . . ." he said.

They held their thumbs together for a moment. She closed her eyes.

She wished that she didn't feel like she was standing in a spot that she'd never be in again, with him wanting her, asking her to stay. She wished she didn't feel the weight of how much her life would change in another week. She wished things could be easier.

They pulled their thumbs apart, revealing whose thumb had the eyelash.

Whose wish it was that would come true.

Makenzie blew the eyelash off of her thumb and repeated all the wishes in her head. But she knew deep down that she had already lost her wish by wishing for too many things at once.

The fireworks started over the blackest sky, and she knew that no matter how hard she wished, the carnival was over.

Summer was over.

It was all over.

Love is the only thing that can never, ever, die.
    It's eternal.

It might be hard to feel it now, because you feel like everything
in the world was dead to you the moment they were gone.

And in a way, you feel like you wish you never loved at all—but
you can't protect the past.
    And in your mind you're reserving all of your future love
already—but you can't safeguard the future.

You just have to keep loving, even though it hurts.
And remember that it's the only way you can stay alive now.
    Because everything dies.
        {Except love.}

. . . .

In the house that isn't mine, it's a revolving door of friends coming and going. It's hard to look some of them in the eyes, but when I do they always hug me afterwards. They can see my pain spilling over, and they are always trying to plug the tears leaking out of me, like holes in a faulty dam, with hugs. These friends tell me how they will all be there for me tomorrow and what time they will arrive, as if her death has an rsvp on the funeral invitation and I'm reserving seats.

I sit back down and I stare at nothing. Until I feel like something's missing, other than the constant aching for her, and I look around the room.

I am able to look at faces and focus just enough to see that none of them are his.

And it's confirmation that part of her is still with me. Because I just want to see him right now. So I walk outside to the small concrete porch just big enough to hold a flower bench and a tall cylindrical Marlboro ashtray.

I see him sitting there alone, just starting to burn a cigarette, and I sit down next to him, next to her boy.

He was always her boy.

Even if he didn't know it.

Everyone else knew it.

And now he will be hers forever.

He offers me the pack and I take one, carefully, as if I'm choosing a winner.

We say nothing.

Until I light my cigarette.

187

Once my cigarette is fueled to burn, I lean forward on my lap, nervously flicking the lighter in my hand past my knees. Then I say, "It's not fair, you know." And I bring my other hand up to catch the cigarette from my lips as I exhale, "you sitting out here just getting two packs of cigarettes closer to seeing her again," and he offers me a slight smile. In my mind I'm already jealous of him or anyone else who might be the next to see her again.

I suck through the filter end of the cigarette as if it's a race. I know the taste of these cigarettes should be harsher than the menthols I'm used to, but there's something about death that makes everything taste the same.

He looks down at the ground. And I watch the smoke float above us. The smoke swirls up past the brown shingled roof of the house that isn't mine before disappearing into the overcast sky.

I look at him.
He's struck by her.
But like me, he knows that it is yet to hit harder.
Maybe in a week.
    Maybe in a month.
But sometime later on, it'll hurt even more than it does now. He knows that, and he tells me how much it sucks—as he's sucking on the end of his cigarette. And I agree, well aware of my own guarded alertness for when it will hurt even more.

And I know he could never forget her.
But I tell him anyways. "You know she's a part of you . . . you'll always have her."
He exhales thick white nicotine-scented clouds and he slowly nods his head. He puts his arm around me, and he squeezes me in as if to thank me for saying so.
"I know . . ." he says.

And for now, at least I have him. At least there is someone whose pain is similar to mine.
And we sit in silence.
His cigarette is done.
    It's ended.

And although mine has ended too and I know that the next drag will only be burnt filter, I can't help but take one last stinging draw into my lungs. The only thing worse than the pain of something ending, is the pain in trying to let go of an end.

He holds his cigarette butt in front of his face and I wonder what he's thinking as he looks at it longingly before pushing it into the top of the ashtray.

He reaches in his shirt pocket to pull out the pack of Marlboro Reds. "Just one more," he says as he puts a new cigarette between his lips. I hold up his lighter, flicking a spark into a flame and reaching it over to the dried tobacco peeking out of the end of his cigarette.

And I nod.

I know what he means.

I wish I had just one more day with her too.

Faith

She sat on the floor of her room feeling all the heaviness of the nighttime starting and the summertime ending. There was no worse feeling than the night falling on an August day. School would start again soon and Makenzie would be starting over somewhere new. Faith didn't want to think about how much she'd miss her best friend. She didn't want to think about how much being left behind would hurt.

Faith sat on her bedroom floor, picking at the mess of belongings that were closest to her, a pile of unlaundered clothes, a loose stack of magazines, some books, and scattered art supplies. She picked up one of the books and a red piece of charcoal as Makenzie started to apply mascara across from the door-length mirror.

". . . that waterproof mascara?" Faith asked, squinting, as if she could have read the tiny text on the tube from across the room.

"No, maybe I shouldn't put a lot on then . . . I don't want to tell everyone I'm moving and then have them remember me by the long black streaks on my face." Makenzie talked slowly so as not to startle her reflection while she swiped the mascara wand across each eyelid's lashes.

"Yeah, I don't think it really matters though, did you ever notice how you can swim in a pool with waterproof mascara all day and be fine, but if one tear leaks out it's streak-city? I think that's why they don't call it 'tear-proof' mascara." Faith concentrated on spreading the charcoal across the pages of the book in her lap.

Makenzie turned to Faith with an eyelash curler closed over her right eye, "Do you think I'm doing the right thing, Fay, I mean what if I tell everyone tonight and they think it's the wrong thing to move. What if they think I'm making a mistake? Do you still think it's the right thing, I mean, I'm not wrong am I, Faith?"

"No, Mazie, you know this is the right thing to do, or you wouldn't be doing it. It'll be fine. It'll be better than fine. You're going to have a family that loves you and I bet your mom will give you a key to that house instead of always locking you out, and they will take you to school and ask how your day is and they will do things that parents are supposed to do instead of berating you all the time. You'll be part of a real family down there, instead of being treated like a guest who outstayed her welcome. I bet you they will even make a big deal out of your birthday and stuff like that. It'll be good, you know it'll be better . . ."

"I know, Fay, I'm just scared, I mean, what if all these things I'm leaving . . . what if I'll never have these things again . . ." Makenzie held her arms out.

"Hey, I know you feel like you're leaving everyone, but there isn't anything or anybody that won't be right here for you to come back to. You're going to come back to these things, Maize, you're not leaving everything, you're just getting a new home." Faith cocked her head to the side and raised her eyebrows, "NO Regrets, okay?"

"You're right, in another year you and everyone else will be off to college ahead of me and I'll be by myself anyways." Makenzie sounded relieved thinking about leaving people before they could leave her.

"That's not what I was talking about, and I'm not going to college, Mazie." Faith continued her sketch in her lap, pulling her knees up to hide it from Makenzie.

"Fay." Makenzie said in a tone like a mother ending a discussion with a child where the child was wrong. "And plus if I stay here how am I going to ever go to college or get a car, or anything. My mom said she'd help with all those things down there, and member when we went to visit and she cooked dinner and we all ate it at the table like a family. I bet you she cooks dinner every night and they all look at each other and smile; they were all smiling at dinner you know?"

"Yeah they were," Faith co-signed the memory trying not to rush Makenzie's beauty process and focusing on filling in her doodle.

"It's just . . . ." Makenzie set down her makeup bag, "What if we're wrong?"

Faith couldn't think like that.

And she couldn't let Makenzie think like that.

"We're not wrong, okay? And even if we *are* wrong . . . *about everything* . . . then these are the things that are going to make us who we are, okay . . . ? And we don't regret who we are now, so we can't regret who we'll become . . ." Faith flipped the book around like a kindergarten teacher sharing a picture book with her students, to show what she had been sketching.

In big charcoal and red block letters, across the page, Faith had doodled,

NO REGRETS

and Faith held her eyebrows raised as if they were an exclamation point accompanying the sketch.

A smile stretched across Makenzie's lips and her face finally looked as beautiful as she had been trying to make it. "That's perfect, Fay. Don't let me regret anything, I don't want to feel like that. Promise you'll remind me when I need it?"

"Of course, I'll always remind you, that's my job!" Faith smiled at Makenzie reassuring her that everything would be okay.

Faith started to close the book but Makenzie stopped her, "Wait! Let's sign it like a contract in blood, then we will always have this as our reminder and then neither of us can break it. Ever." Makenzie said.

Faith laughed, but Makenzie was serious. So serious that she had already zipped up her makeup bag and was combing Faith's dresser for a pointy object.

"Do you have any safety pins or anything . . . ?" Makenzie looked around.

Faith pointed to one on her dresser for Makenzie to use and Makenzie looked like she was hoping Faith would go first.

"Wait!" Faith stopped Makenzie in mid-poke, "Maybe we should sterilize it right? With a lighter or something?" Makenzie nodded in agreement and reached in the front pocket of her jean skirt for her lighter.

She flicked the Bic lighter and the flame covered most of the safety pin turning it a charred color of dark brown. Makenzie shrugged her shoulders and tried to jab herself again without drawing any blood, "Ah! It's so hot! I can't get anything."

"Here," Faith reached for the safety pin and tried to pierce her unsuspecting pointer finger. Nothing. "Fuck that hurts, still burns from the flame."

"Lemme try again . . ." Makenzie slowly took the safety pin back and tried pushing it into her skin but could only get so far. "Shit. This isn't working." Makenzie looked at the time, "Oh man, it's already a quarter after eleven, the boys will be here soon . . ."

Makenzie ditched the safety pin and as Faith was about to close the book Makenzie said "Wait." She went over to her makeup bag sitting in front of the mirror.

Faith watched Makenzie put on a heavy layer of bright red lipstick before she handed Faith the tube. Faith shook her head looking at the extended red tube, thinking about how much she would never wear red lipstick especially just going out with the boys. But then Makenzie pulled the book close to her face and kissed the page under "REGRETS." Makenzie looked at Faith, smiling.

Faith rubbed on more red-colored whale fat than she ever had in her whole life and kissed the page opposite Makenzie's under "NO."

It was a deal.
It was a promise.
It was a contract, almost in blood.

{No Regrets.}

There are no coincidences.
There are no accidents.

There are only dots that you must connect to reveal that you are in a greater picture, and that you are part of a grander plan. You might not be able to see the finished mosaic that is your life right now, but you must trust that even the broken pieces will, in the end, connect to create something beautiful.

· · · · · · · ·

I wait for this day to fade like I imagine I'll be waiting for all the rest of my life to fade. And I realize that I still have the piece of round metal in my hand, suctioned to my palm, and that I've forgotten to write to her about it.

So I grab my notebook.

The front of the peach notebook now has a photo of us taped to the cover. The girl with the soft voice helped me cut the photo into the shape of a heart. The photo says a thousand words, but cutting it into the shape of the heart says only one—Love.

I peel past the sad used-up pages to a new fresh one. And I start to write.

"Hey Best Friend,

Yesterday the boys and I went down to your spot. The last spot that you ever lived. It was just me and the boy with the motorcycle and the boy with the baseball hat. The other guys wanted to come, but, I think it was too much for them. But I needed to see it. I wanted to see the last place you were and I wanted to hear the last thing that you heard. We rode to the spot in the Camaro, just like when we picked you up for the homecoming dance. Except this time the back seat of that car felt lonely without you.

I felt my phone vibrate over the loud music and it was a text from the boy with the motorcycle from the front seat. It just said, "I love you."

He's never said that to me before . . .

It must just be because you're not here to say it to me—so he thinks he ought to.

I could feel it coming as we got closer, my stomach dropped and my heart twisted up into my throat. I knew exactly where the spot was as soon as we got to it. We pulled over and saw the flowers in the grass median between the highways. We could see the stains of blood and car fluids on the road. The tire marks really creeped me out the most. How are they still there, so many days later, and you're not? It's so fucked up. The grass was plowed down with tire marks where you went off, and I just sat down next to them. Sobbing at first but then I just couldn't take it and I got so scared, not for me, but for you. I'm so sorry that I wasn't there . . . I can't believe that I let you go through that alone. I'll be apologizing forever, you know . . .

I put the cross that I made for you into the ground and I held on to it crying so loud over all the noise of the highway. I wrote on the cross with markers, your name and the date, and on the other side I wrote "No Regrets."

Once it was in the ground, I couldn't stop crying. It felt final . . . the way that I guess it will feel tomorrow when they put you in the ground. I hate thinking about that now. It's too much to think about all at once.

The tractor trailers that went by on the highway were so loud. They were so heavy. They were so fucking . . . scary. Every time one went by I felt the wind of it almost knock me over. The vibrations from the tires on those trucks went through the road and right through me. I couldn't stop shaking from the trucks. The sounds of little cars went by like bullets, and they all pushed more tears out of me than I even thought I had left. I just sat there in the grass absorbing every sound and every bit of pain.

The boys went over to look at the marks on the road and they tried to piece together what might have happened. I didn't need to know though. Knowing won't change what it is now.

When I walked over to where they were, there was so much broken glass and little pieces of shredded metal on the side of the road, like the worst kind of glitter, but it just made me think of you, shining the way you always did. And that's when I found the metal emblem from your car, cradled in the grass in between black pieces of plastic. I picked it up and it fit perfectly in the palm of my hand. I like the way it feels in my hand. Kind of like you're holding my hand back, but kinda like if I keep my hand over it then maybe I can go back in time and my hand will be there to shield everything . . . or at least my body would be in front of the car and I could have gone with you.

And then the boy with the motorcycle noticed that my finger was bleeding. Maybe I cut it on some of the glass shards picking up the emblem, or maybe it was from the wood of the cross while I was holding on to it so tightly, I dunno . . . it didn't hurt, I couldn't feel it, but I was so glad for the blood.

Because it reminded me.

I felt like you were there telling me that it's okay.

To finish our pact.

And I ran back to the cross, against the wind from all of the tractor trailers and cars pushing me back and I knelt down next to it. Next to the road that your blood was on, I pushed my bloody finger against the dry wood of the cross, and smeared it under where it said "No Regrets."

I know you were there.

I know you already know, it's official now.

And I know you're keeping your promise. Because, I know you have no regrets where you are now. Heaven can't possibly have room for things like regret.

And I'll try hard not to have any down here.

I promise.

Makenzie

The day Makenzie finished packing to leave was the worst day of her life. All she wanted to do was to stay in one place and to not feel like a burden to anyone. She hated having to explain her plans to move to anyone. She hated it more when people asked her to stay. She didn't want to rip herself from everyone, she didn't want to be the drama queen or the bad guy, but she couldn't find the words to explain to them that there was a feeling inside her louder than all of the pleas to stay. There was this feeling that she just had to go and that if she didn't listen to it, she might just explode with more than just tears. There was this level of anxiety about not leaving that didn't make sense. But the only thoughts that calmed her were when she would think about starting out somewhere new.

She had to do it.

And it was okay if no one understood why.

She packed up everything important to her, pictures came off of the walls and her room looked like an empty prison cell. She didn't own enough suitcases to uproot herself in style. Instead all of her clothes and belongings were in bloated black trash bags. She felt nauseated at the thought of her life being reduced to trash in that moment.

"Here, lemme get those," Faith reached her hands out to grab one trash bag with each arm and Makenzie took a deep breath.

"Hold on a minute." Makenzie couldn't catch her thoughts. She couldn't stop the moments from happening. She couldn't believe that she was actually leaving. She was about to go downstairs and leave her dad. The thing that she had been planning to do this whole time, she never actually wanted to do. She just wanted to be closer to him, like it used to be. But as long as he was remarried and starting a new life, it was never going to be just the two of them like it was before. She was never going to belong to his new family. It would never be the same again. But one day, she knew she could at least belong to him in a better way. Even though that meant leaving now. Maybe instead of screaming curse words at each other they would meet for coffee one day. And she knew if she ever wanted to sit in a coffee shop across from him with a soy latte in her hand and tell him about her day, that she had to leave now.

The rebuilding had to start with a complete demolition of the old.

An emotional implosion.

She tried to simmer her thoughts and not let them boil over. But what hurt her the most about leaving was knowing that her dad would have never left her. Never. He had fought for her years ago. He had fought just to keep her. She knew that. She felt like she had betrayed her mom back then. And she felt like she was betraying her dad now. And she hated that it had to be like that. Because to her, them not being together felt like they had been the ones to betray her.

She never wanted this.

Why did she have to have all the guilt of choosing sides when it was their fault that the pain even existed? Why did she have to take the blame? She didn't want to hurt anyone, but this wasn't about her mom or her dad right now. It was about this house.

It was always about this house and how she didn't belong there.

"Okay . . . I'm ready." Makenzie put on her black sunglasses with pink flames on the sides and took in one last filtered look at the life she was leaving behind.

She dragged the trash bag down the stairs and stopped at the door. She turned to her left to say, "Goodbye, Dad"

And he said "See ya."

But she knew he wouldn't be seeing her.
She hadn't been seen in years.

Grief has no rules.
But there is one piece of advice that it whispers.
If you listen, you can hear it through the rising smoke of death.
  It's saying,
  "Keep moving. Don't look back. No regrets."

. . . .

A car wreck.

Those exact words that define her death now simultaneously describe my whole life.

Everyone is grieving.
    Everyone.
But in different ways.
Until now, the only reference I've ever known to "grief" has been from Charlie Brown. And I don't know why he ever said it was good . . .
    It's not.
      At all.
It's hard, and it's confusing. It's like the worst secret society anyone can be in. You only find out about it once you're initiated. You can only talk about it with other people who have been through the humiliating life hazing of losing someone so close. I wish that someone would have told me at the start of all this that going through grief means not only losing someone, but that every moment would be a fight for something. Every day I'm losing more of her and more of myself.

I barely slept at all last night. Friends came over to the house that isn't mine, we painted our nails black, even the boy with the motorcycle let us paint his toenails for her, partly to make us smile and partly I'm sure so he wouldn't forget the piece of his soul that was now black from her leaving.
We sat. With painted nails. And we listened to the saddest music ever written. It was the worst sleepover of my entire life. Maybe this is why grown-ups don't have sleepovers. Cause it's just all gross and sad.

Now with solemn faces and tired eyes we all try to get ready for the funeral. We just wait together, quietly, for it to be time to leave. And it feels like I'll always be waiting to leave. For the rest of my life I will feel like I'm just waiting to leave and to get where she is.

I can feel the couch below me hug me back and I think about how this house that isn't mine was always home base. There wasn't a time in my memory when this house ever held less than two friends and when more weren't already on their way over.

I think about all the memories.

I look around the living room at faces of friends that I wouldn't have if it weren't for this house. And I think about all of the times, good and bad, when each person in this room needed this house like I need it now. This house has held all of us together when our worlds were falling apart. I wish I could just stay in this house forever.

But I know that we have to leave.

Everyone has to leave.

Eventually.

The door from the hallway swings open and shuts behind the boy with the goatee. He walks out from his back bedroom, adjusting his tie and sits down next to me on his couch.

He holds his right palm face up expecting a low-five. What used to be a slap-happy greeting before an adventure is now just his way of saying that he's here for me. And I quietly wipe my hand across his like the weakest, saddest, low-five there ever was because I've never been so low in my life as I am now.

And I'm not ready for this.

I think about a thousand moments in time before this when we all would be sitting in this house, just like this, with nothing better to do.

But we will never be those same bored, stupid kids again.

Now we sit here with serious faces, in suits and skirts looking like we all could be headed to a freaking business meeting or something. Death dressed us up like we are all waiting to apply for a job in the darkest cubicles of Hell.

As we sit, I look down at myself covered in black and I look around at everyone else sitting around and they are wearing different shades of gray with the darkest hues of colors. I think about the last time she was in this house with all of us and we were doing the exact same thing, we were waiting to leave, but we were leaving for Graduation.

I reach in my memory and it feels like forever ago, but it was only four short weeks that everyone was wearing bright colors and white gowns sitting in the exact same seats. I remember taking pictures and listening to silly stories.

I remember her laughing.

I remember myself laughing.

I remember how bright the future seemed that day for everyone. Like anything and everything was ours.

And now, the future's so dim that I can't see past today.

It doesn't feel like we have anything now.

It still looks like everything has always been hers all along.

Makenzie

Makenzie went into the upstairs bathroom at her new house, and she didn't want to do it, but she had to.

She inched the puckered piece of metal in the center of the door handle from horizontal to vertical.

And she sighed as she turned to look at the toilet by the window.

She hadn't even met this toilet yet, and their first encounter was going to be ass-backwards. Just like her life right now.

Makenzie bent down to the base of the toilet, looking around at all the extra special details the bathroom had at her mom's house. The shower curtain matching the bath rug, the soap on the counter sink matching the hand towel, the toilet paper holder with extras waiting in the wings.

And as Makenzie bent over the toilet, she could smell how clean it was.

It was fresh. Her mom had probably run bleach over everything before Makenzie came making sure her new life would be spotless.

And Makenzie felt something in her stomach that reminded her of failure as she wondered if she would ever be perfect enough.

Either way, Makenzie didn't think that her mom ever imagined what Makenzie would be doing in this bathroom. How could she. Makenzie lied to people even when they straight up asked her if she was bulimic. She would panic at the question.

She hated lying, but what could she really tell people. She couldn't tell people the truth. She couldn't tell everyone who loved her that she just needed to throw up to stay balanced in an unbalanced world. Maybe she could find people to tell in her new school. Maybe it would just become a part of who she was and she wouldn't have to hide it. But what would she say, *"Hi, I'm Makenzie I moved down here because my life is totally fucked up and p.s. I'm bulimic."* And even if she had the courage to say that, what if people didn't understand.

People not understanding her would make it worse, it would feel that the courage was all for nothing. That she was the problem and not bulimia. Or even worse, that bulimia didn't exist. Makenzie knew how people thought about it. They wouldn't say it, but they would think it—that it's all in her head. But it wasn't just in her head.

That was the scariest part.

It was everywhere inside of her.

Her body ached with the need to throw up like her bones ached with the need to crack. And going a day without cracking her knuckles, or her neck, or her back, was just the same now as if she went a few days without throwing up. Her body wouldn't let her forget. It was constantly reminding her of it.

Her stomach popped up a little burst of air, a small burp, while she was tying her hair back. Her body knew. She no longer had to tell her body when it was time, her body now told her.

And she leaned over the cleanest toilet she had ever seen and without even really trying to, she spilt out what was inside of her like a coffee cup that was just a touch too full. The hot acid burned what it touched.

Anymore, the vomit was always a pinkish orange color. This time, it was more pinkish red—from more blood coming up. One small drop of blood from the back of her throat would spread in the toilet like a drop of red food coloring. It didn't surprise Makenzie anymore. Every other time now, there would be blood.

Every purge now felt like she had swallowed a cheese grater and it was constantly working up and down the insides of her throat.
And now, because of it, her body was a walking, talking, breathing open wound.

Slowly being re-opened again and again.

Food particles and acid ripping and digging into the lining of her esophagus. Clawing a path of destruction up and out what should have only ever been a one-way road for food to go down and in. Everything coming back up the wrong direction was fighting gravity, fighting digestion, fighting life.

Her body was always fighting.

She was always fighting something.

Faith

She woke up at Makenzie's new house to Makenzie blow drying her wet hair. Visiting Makenzie on weekends had become a new, but an old routine. A part of growing up meant they wouldn't have sleepovers at Grandma's house anymore but it didn't mean they had to stop having sleepovers all together. Best friends would always have sleepovers, plus they talked about getting an apartment together, which would mean sleepovers every night until they got married.

But all Faith could think about now was sleep. Faith tried falling back asleep, but Makenzie instigated the morning.

"Good morning, Sunshine!" Makenzie put down the hair dryer and danced around the edge of the bed. Faith never understood how at 7:30 in the morning on a Saturday it was possible for anyone to be dancing.

"Makenzie." Faith let out an oh-my-god-please-let-me-go-back-to-sleep grunt and rolled over to the cool side of Makenzie's extra pillow.

"C'mon, Fay!" Makenzie slapped Faith's blanket-covered butt just once like she was starting a horse to gallop, "Mom's making your favorite!"

Faith could smell the cinnamon rolls almost at the exact same moment that Makenzie had confirmed they were in the oven. "Good, save me one," Faith talked into her pillow, eyes closed.

"C'mon . . ." Makenzie brushed at her strawberry blonde hair, ". . . I have a surprise for you . . . the boys are downstairs! They drove out last night and stayed in the spare room! They're already at the table, everyone's waiting for you!" Faith could hear Makenzie's feet bouncing as she talked.

"Nah-uh?" Faith didn't believe it, but she wouldn't put it past the boys to drive all night somewhere just for breakfast, they had once all driven an hour and a half just to go to the Waffle House before. She rolled over, opened her eyes, and looked at Makenzie for her response.

"Aha! Your eyes are open, you're up now! C'mon!" Makenzie pointed at Faith's awkward morning face.

"Are they really here?" Faith used her pillow to help her sit up.

"Nope! But you are now!" Makenzie laughed at her success at a near-impossible feat.

Faith sighed, made a face that ended in a smile, and threw a pillow across the room at Makenzie.

Makenzie pounced out of the way laughing and danced around the cinnamon-bun-smelling-room, excited for the day.

Makenzie

She sat in the passenger seat of Faith's car and it felt different than all the times before. The seat didn't feel like it was hers anymore, like nobody else would ever sit there. She looked over at Faith and noticed how labored her driving was. Faith was using the steering wheel to pull herself closer to the windshield as if she were driving through a shit storm.

"Do you know where you're going?" Makenzie asked thinking about how all her new friends could drive these streets of Maryland with one hand on the wheel and one eye on the road, relaxed.

"Yeah . . . I think so, it's just on the left up here, right? After that sharp turn?" Faith spoke to Makenzie without letting her eyes leave the road.

"Yup. I'll tell you when to turn." Makenzie looked at the rows of corn that lined the streets beside her and wondered if this place she was in would ever feel like home. She wondered if starting over was really what she needed to do. If she was really supposed to be here.

"Hey Mazie, look at that billboard up there. What the heck is that, do you know? Is it like something coming to this spot that they're advertising?" Faith pointed to the right of the steering wheel and touched the windshield of the car with her right pointer finger.

"I don't know, what's it say?" Makenzie squinted.

"It says *HERE* and that's all it says. Why wouldn't it even have a phone number if you wanted to advertise on it, it's like "HERE" is the advertisement or something, what the hell?" Faith giggled like the entire state of Maryland was on crack.

"Here . . ." As they got closer, Makenzie could see the thick black letters, all surrounded by clean empty white space. She had never seen that billboard before, it must have been new. She grabbed her camera out of her purse and rolled down the window as they approached the sign.

Maybe it really was a sign.

Maybe Makenzie needed a sign that big to remind her that even in all her doubt that she was supposed to be "here". Maybe she just needed to trust the flow of life and look for the messages along the way.

{HERE}

She leaned out the window and she took a picture.

Faith

"Are you going to get a soy latte?" Faith asked, squinting at the coffee shop's chalkboard, deciding what she would get.

"Oh no, actually, Fay I want a hot chocolate." Makenzie held on to paper and pens to get an early start on Christmas cards. Faith smiled, it was barely Thanksgiving but she knew how excited Makenzie was to send Christmas cards from her new address. She had so much to say to everyone.

"Sounds good. I think I'll get one too." Faith nodded her head.

"I miss drinking hot chocolate with you, man." Makenzie made a sad face, and Faith elbowed her and rolled her eyes with a smile.

"Well, it's happening!" Faith teased Makenzie as she stepped one person closer to the counter in the barista's line.

"No really!" Makenzie got serious, "Really Fay, It's one of those things, thinking about this coming winter, and how much I miss everyone. And I've already decided that's going to be my Christmas present to everyone this year, two packs of instant hot cocoa wrapped up in a bow, because the best gift in life is just having someone to drink hot chocolate with."

"Aw that's thoughtful, Mazie, I bet everyone will love them." Faith took another step closer to the counter envisioning the bow Makenzie would tie around the two packets, well knowing that some people Makenzie gifted this year would wonder what they were missing, if hot chocolate was some kind of inside joke or some new beauty remedy. Most people wouldn't think that having hot chocolate was the best gift in life. Some people just wouldn't get it, even after Makenzie explained it. Because most people don't appreciate the people they have in their life, let alone appreciate drinking hot chocolate with them, not the way Makenzie did. And she stepped up to say, "Two hot chocolates please."

"Extra whipped cream!" Makenzie added, making sure to make eye contact with the barista when she said "extra." Faith held her debit card out and Makenzie said, "I'll grab us a seat," as she juggled her things.

Faith set the hot chocolates down on a small round tabletop, a cardboard sleeve around each one holding in some of the heat that was slowly escaping from the small adult-sip-cup-like-coffee-lid-opening.

"Careful, it's really hot."

"Really? The hot chocolate . . .? Say it ain't so . . ." Makenzie teased Faith without even glancing up from the stack of Christmas cards she had in front of her.

Faith pulled a few loose Christmas cards out of her tote bag and dug for a pen. Faith wasn't that into writing Christmas cards, but Makenzie had insisted that she bring some to write too, so she did. Faith didn't really know the kind of thing you wrote about in Christmas cards. Faith looked over at Makenzie, her pen barely even lifted from the paper it just kept going and going. Makenzie was writing so much. But Faith wasn't sure she even had anything to say other than "Merry Christmas" and maybe throw in something about the new year coming up and how great it should be. Faith sighed trying hard not to think about Christmas or the New Year, and she took a sip of hot chocolate.

"So who is that one for?" Faith asked over the steam of her hot chocolate, her eyes pointing to the card in front of Makenzie covered in ink.

"This one . . . this one's for my dad." Makenzie looked up at Faith, with eyes that begged not to be judged.

"Did he ever email you back?" Faith asked Makenzie what the latest communication with him even was, knowing very well that if someone didn't want to be contacted, eventually it just has to be accepted.

"Yeah." Makenzie said softly.

"Oh. Okay."

"It was just a short email, though. I dunno . . ." Makenzie looked up at her cooling hot chocolate before looking at Faith, "I just have so much to say to him, and he has like only a few words to say to me . . ."

"Well, I'm not sure what you expect from him . . . you're the one who left, remember? He probably is just giving you space. Maybe he just doesn't know what you want him to say to you. I mean . . . what do you want him to say anyways?"

"I dunno, Faith, maybe that he's sorry how things turned out, that I left. Maybe just say that he loves me." Makenzie lifted her hot chocolate and blew slowly into the small opening of the lid pushing the steam that was coming out, back in.

"Sorry, Mazie, you know he loves you though." Faith took a sip. Of course Makenzie's dad had to love her, but Faith's expectation of fathers in general was jaded. She knew that because of that, what she just said didn't sound convincing.

"Yeah . . ." Makenzie looked off towards the door of the coffee shop.

The sounds of chatter, clicking laptop keyboards, and the clinking of plates with scones were all around them.

"Hey Fay . . . do you ever think about writing a card . . . or a letter . . . to your dad?" Makenzie held her hot chocolate in front of her with both hands cupped around it.

"Yeah . . ." Faith slowly nodded her head in a way that begged her eyes not to water.

"So why haven't you?"

"I did. I mean, I wrote a letter a bit ago . . . there's just nowhere to send it to," Faith shrugged and tried to push out a little laugh. She looked down into the lid of her hot chocolate at the little drops of cocoa that had escaped from the inside and were now loose in the curves of the plastic lid and finding themselves a way out.

"What'd . . . what'd you say . . . ?" Makenzie's face was filled with more worry than wonder.

"Everything I needed to. And you know what, I felt better. It's like Grandma always says, you've got to get it all out, write it down, and throw it away if you have to, but you've got to get it out. "

"Yeah . . ." Makenzie took another sip.

"So . . . even if you don't send that card, make sure it's filled with everything you need to say. Don't keep all the shitty feelings you have inside, just because someone else doesn't want to hear it. " Faith felt relieved, like she was giving Makenzie solid advice.

"Yeah. You're right." Makenzie set down her hot chocolate and picked her pen back up. Before she started she asked Faith again, "So what all did your letter say though?"

". . . ummm . . ." Faith paused, not to remember what the letter said—those feelings merged into every breath of every day—but she needed to pause to find a way to say the words out loud. "Well . . . I told him about how sick I am. And how mad I was that he wasn't there for me when I needed him the most. I told him how I cried every night after he left . . . for months. I told him how much he fucked up. That he broke my trust and my heart . . . and I asked him what was so goddamn important . . . what was so much more important than me that he had to leave . . ."

Faith tried not to let even a single tear fall. She didn't need some random Starbucks by Makenzie's house in Maryland to be stained with the stupid memories of her dad leaving her in Pennsylvania, but that's the way it fucking went.

It followed her everywhere and even if she didn't talk about it, or say it out loud ever, the truth was that Faith knew for the rest of her life, every person, every place, every future moment would eventually, somehow be tarnished by the pain of her past.

". . . I told him that I hoped he found whatever he was missing. And that I hope whatever it was, that it was worth all the things that he took away from me."

"Wow . . . Faith . . ." Makenzie's eyes were full and she blinked twice to see Faith better.

". . . And then, at the end . . . I told him I forgive him for it all. I forgive him for all the things he missed, and for all the future things he'll miss . . . and for all that I'm forever missing because of him. All the times in the future that I will be less . . . that I will *feel* less . . . all of those things are his fault . . . but I forgive him."

Makenzie's eyes looked shocked and so Faith continued, "I'm not saying it's okay now. Forgiving him doesn't mean what he did was okay, it just…it's because….I don't need the pain of holding onto it. You can't hold onto other people's mistakes. You have to let them go . . ."

Faith shrugged her shoulders.

Don't be ashamed of your struggle.
    Do not let the pain make you bitter.
    Do not let your sadness shut you down.

You may be broken now, but if you can only know one thing, know that these struggles are not your weakness.

    These struggles are where your strength is born.

. . . .

I carry baskets of picture frames into the Funeral Home and scatter them as quickly as I can around the tables and desks so when people come in they see her first, smiling. I have this awful twisting feeling in my stomach like I am setting up for the worst reverse surprise party ever. The one where the guest of honor enters the room first, dead in a casket. And we are the only ones surprised.

People start to trickle in through the wooden doors with decorated glass set into them. It's not a church, but the heavy doors, the serious air, and the pending judgment remind me exactly of a church.

There are people that look like they are glad to see me.
But how can they be.
When I'm not her.
I try to understand their loving looks, but I can't.
I just can't.
I feel ashamed.
Because I can't help but feel like I am just what's left.
A consolation prize.
The dud.

But they still hug me harder than I've ever been hugged in my life. Hugs so hard that I feel like I could fall apart between their arms. I almost feel comfort until I realize that these hugs aren't for me.
They are for the lack of her.

And then it becomes clear through my grieving haze that all of this love is just their way of freeing themselves from the guilt of the love that they couldn't give to her whether it be in the past, the present, or the future.

And this is *my* consolation prize.

But deep down, I know that they have to be wishing that she were here instead of me.
     I know.
     And I don't blame them.
          Because I can't stop wishing it too.

Makenzie

"So how was your day, tell me what happened." Faith asked through the phone line.

"It was okay, I made some new friends that seem pretty cool, we are going to hang out this weekend." Makenzie sounded slightly hopeful about starting a second semester at her new school.

"Oh well that's good, hey, are you getting sick or something your voice sounds hoarse." Faith worried about her through the phone. Makenzie didn't want to admit that her voice was hoarse because her throat was sore, and that her throat was sore from all the acid washing up from her stomach. Her throat was always in pain anymore.

"I dunno, maybe."

"How was the rest of the day, did you have any problems? Were you okay today?" Faith asked and Makenzie knew exactly what she meant by "okay." Faith meant was Makenzie able to create enough willpower inside her to not let the bulimia and anxiety-ridden thoughts take hold of her guts that day.

"I was okay, I only threw up once," Makenzie admitted. "Just the one time though and it hurt like hell." Makenzie sounded disgusted but proud of herself at the same time for only giving in once to thoughts that beckoned a thousand times a day. Only once, and even though there was pain, it still felt like a silver medal.

Faith was just disappointed, "Man, Mazie, you were doing so good, why did you feel like you had to today, what was different?" The question made Makenzie realize the frequency of purging really had increased. She used to have a streak of days, weeks even, when she didn't feel strangled by thoughts to purge. Now they were there as soon as she woke up and sometimes they kept her up at night. She was eating better since she moved in with her mom and she was exercising more, but none of that seemed to take any power away from the bulimia.

It was getting worse.

"I dunno, just couldn't stop the feeling." Makenzie didn't even know how to identify her own triggers yet, and certainly didn't know how to explain them to someone else.

"I hate it. I hate being so far away and not being able to help you; how would you feel if I just stopped taking my meds?"

"Faith. Stop it." Makenzie couldn't count the number of times that she had called Faith to make sure she was taking her medicine on time, she was already worried about her not taking doses without her there.

"How would you feel?! You'd feel exactly as helpless and upset as I feel. I'm not taking my medicine today now." Faith sounded like a snob.

"Faith, quit it. This isn't about you, you need your medicine to stay healthy." The last thing Makenzie needed was a more disappointment.

"And you need to keep food down to stay healthy. So, what? You care more about my health than you do about yours, well guess what I care more about your health than I do about mine. So I'm not taking medicine on days that you throw up and you can freaking sit on it. If you don't care what you're doing to yourself maybe you'll care if you can see what it does to me." Faith's voice started to crack.

"Fay that's not fair, please just take your medicine today. I'm already upset about it now." Makenzie could stand letting herself down, she was used to that feeling, but she couldn't stand letting Faith down.

"Fine." Faith's sigh continued as her words fell, "but I swear to God that's the deal for next time. Now you know it's what I'm going to do. And you can't be mad at me then."

Makenzie hated her ultimatum.

Mostly because she could never lie to Faith.

"Alright . . . alright," Makenzie unwillingly agreed.

"Hey . . . I'm still proud of you for only doing it once though," Faith encouraged her. "Why don't you put on some music and get your charcoals out and draw me a picture. I have an empty space on my wall and it just opened its mouth to tell me that it needs some more Makenzie originals."

And Makenzie instinctively nodded even though Faith couldn't see, knowing how much putting any amount of charcoal to paper made her feel more like herself. Drawing made her feel less stressed. It made her feel accomplished in a way that nothing else did.

"Sure, Fay, coming right up," and Makenzie smiled thinking about how being able to control the direction of the pencil strokes, in even a doodle, made her feel like she had more control of her own direction. There was something about controlling the pressure of the pencils on paper, making the weight of the lines go from light to heavy that made her feel less concerned about her own weight. And there was always something about being able to finish a picture, any picture, that made her feel more complete herself.

Art was the outlet that she needed to let all of the pain escape in a way that wouldn't cause more pain. Letting all her emotions out on to the paper in strokes and hard lines made her feel healthy and alive. And as long as she stayed busy, creating something, there was no room for the self-destroying thoughts to come in.

Faith

Another doctor's appointment. And another disappointment. She was going backwards. Backwards with her weight, backwards with her progress, backwards with her treatments.

The medicines weren't working.

She knew they couldn't stop the disease, but they weren't even stopping the symptoms anymore.

The disease was winning.

It meant she had to go back on steroids. Again. She hated prednisone. She never thought she could hate a pill the same size as a ladybug so much.

"Isn't there something else I can take to stop the bleeding? I don't like how the prednisone makes me feel. It makes me feel worse." Faith was sitting in the consult chair at the Children's Hospital, even though she hadn't been a child since the day she had gotten her disease. Her visits were more frequent, and she was three shades paler since her last appointment.

"No, prednisone has shown to have the best success with patients, I know most girls hate how it puffs up their face, I understand . . . even men hate that side effect." The Doctor smiled jovially.

But he didn't understand. The puffy face was nothing. She was experiencing far worse scenarios to care what her freaking face looked like.

She didn't want to have to go back on the medicine because of how it made her feel. It was so strong, it took over her body, mind, and spirit. She hated the agitated way her mind raced on prednisone, how it demanded every ounce of attention from her body. Her eyes always needed to be alert and her limbs jittery, as if the prednisone needed a constant audience for the work that it did to restore her insides. But even when it didn't fix her, because it wasn't a cure, it never stopped breaking the rest of her down. She couldn't sleep on prednisone. Ever. And her thoughts, like her body, would become so exhausted that they would start to become manic. Crazed. Desperate.

Faith panicked, "But," and she realized that the Doctor already had his foot out the door, there was no time to plead for a different medicine. He wouldn't care how she felt, Doctors like him only cared about statistics and results in other people and how the test studies showed she should be feeling. She wished that he could have allowed her the time to tell him everything the prednisone did to her. She wished she could have had the time to tell him that she didn't want it.

That she never wanted any of this.

Faith could only quickly ask, "How long do you think I'd need to take it before . . . how soon will it work?" She sighed, knowing how hard it would be to live for the next few weeks.

The Doctor handed her the scribbled prescription and fixed his pen back into his pocket, "Well, we are going to start you off on 60 mg a day on an eight-week taper, and we'll check in again before the end to see how you're doing. If you're still having the flare-up, we may stretch it out longer and keep you at a lesser milligram for a while." The Doctor spoke fast, like he was on prednisone himself.

Faith didn't think that she could be any more depressed, but now she knew that eight weeks, and then a "mystery while" longer would accomplish that.

Her brain was begging her not to poison it. Her eyes went wide and filled with a layer of tears just thin enough to blur the prescription in her hand.

60 mg . . .

When she took prednisone before she had only taken 40 mg.

There was no way she'd survive a higher dosage of it now.

She was weaker than before.

Not stronger.

Now, it wasn't about surviving the disease, it was about surviving the medicine. They weren't treatments, they were just added torture. The prednisone would sabotage her with a side effect of extreme hunger that would only tear up her insides worse. Having hunger inside her body at the same time as having inflammation inside, made hunger its own disease. It's like being lost in an ocean on a raft with only salt water to survive, except it quickens death by dehydration. Prednisone would put her on her own raft with food all around, making her painfully analyze the contents of each food choice and weigh the payoff of the nutrients of the food versus how quickly it would lead her to the familiar bending over in pain position. Even the blandest most boring of foods like rice, potatoes, and bread would drive her mad with pain. They would all make her bleed more. And maybe it would be worth the pain if the prednisone at least stopped the bleeding, but it didn't.

Because it wasn't a cure.

The steroid was just something that suppressed her immune system, weakening it just enough so it wouldn't keep attacking itself.

The steroid's job was to make her weaker.

But she was already the weakest she had ever been.

Tears of mourning
> *are different than any other tears you will cry.*

> *Tears of heartache hold lessons.*
> *Tears of stress hold relief.*
> *Even tears of disappointment*
> > *hold at least some ounce of hope.*

> *Tears of mourning won't bring the kind of instant release that other kinds of tears do, but you've got to let them out of you, even if they keep coming for the rest of your life.*

> *Because only when they are running down your face,*
> > *can you truly face your grief.*

. . . .

There are people in the Funeral Home crying too loudly and some people not crying at all, and I'm in between.

Like this day.

Like this place.

I'll forever be in a purgatory, stuck between my life and her death.

Someone guides me to a seat, and I see bodies covered in mourning moving towards me. The figures and shapes all look the same, and it's too much to look people in the eye, it burns down deep into my soul like I'm staring into an eclipse. The pain in other people's eyes, especially when they see me, is blinding.

But there are people coming up to me, and giving me their condolences. There are swirls of "I'm sorry's" moving all around me, all followed by an embrace. Some are more filled with their own pain than others.

But I don't know what to say.

Because it's not my loss. I still have her with me. I have the best part of her with me. I can feel it. Still.

It's the entire rest of the universe who never met her who is at loss.

I'm sorry for them. Their lives will undoubtedly suck forever without ever having known her. But I still have her with me. And it's hard to explain how I feel like I'm already carrying her with me, so instead I say just say "thank you," and I return the hugs.

There are people coming up to me whom I haven't seen in months, some people I've never even met. But they are all assuring me how much she loved me. And even though I know . . . it feels so good to hear it.

Because I realize that after today, I may never hear it again.

Ever.

And so I try to take in all of these hugs and this love that people have saved up for her—that they are giving to me now, and my arms quiver. I try to breathe as my legs shake below me, admitting that they aren't strong enough or old enough to wear this black pants suit that I have on.

And I realize that the funeral doesn't feel so much like a goodbye to her as it feels like a census. Like gathering everyone who is still alive into the same room to inventory how they are doing without her and mostly through hugs and teary glances to agree that she is really, in fact, gone.

Because it didn't really feel this real until everyone else said it here today. Not until they all agreed that her life was too short that I felt like her life was really over.

It's really over.

And I hate how the adults at the funeral are so heavy, and they keep referencing how short her life was. As if she didn't even have a chance yet to live. She lived every day. I just have to remind myself that they don't know that. They don't know how alive she really was. That at 2 am these people were asleep the whole time we were alive. She told me herself that she lived more in her life than most people live in a lifetime. She knew it. And I knew it.

I just have to remember her words now, and not theirs as these adults cling to me with condolences.

And what hurts more than the adults in this room thinking that her life was too short, is the thought that I can feel some of them thinking—that she messed up.

She lost control.

She wrecked.

It was her fault.

But I can't entertain those accusations. Even if they all think that she was just a reckless teenager, I know her better than they do. And I know that the only thing that ever made her careless, or clumsy, or weak was that fucking disease.

Maybe she passed out.

Maybe her heart gave out.

But it wasn't because she was wrong.

She was never wrong.

Faith

She sat at Makenzie's new kitchen table and thought about how every time she came down to visit her since Makenzie moved, that she felt better than the last. It was soon to be spring and then summer would come and they could make week-long road trip plans to see each other and friends. There's something about the cold air of winter lifting that just made everything seem like it's going to be alright, like everything could be exciting and new again. And for the first time, Faith felt like Maryland really was where Makenzie was supposed to be.

Makenzie stood in the kitchen unloading the dishwasher while Faith picked at a loose thread on one of the fancy placemats in front of each wooden chair at the dining room table.

"Hey Makenzie, before I leave, let's plan when you can come up next. I'm sure everyone is going to ask me," Faith said while looking around at all the frames on the walls, feeling good knowing that soon Makenzie would be in all the pictures in that house. Faith turned back to look at Makenzie and asked, "Havin' fun with those dishes there?"

"No. Fay" Makenzie said forcefully as she clanked each dish back into its correct cupboard.

"I was just kidding . . . geeze."

"Fay, I can't." Makenzie stopped moving the dishware around and squeezed the drying towel with both hands. Her eyes looked redder than the apples on the counter behind her.

"You can't what? I didn't say tomorrow or next weekend, I said we'll plan a time together whenever." Faith got defensive, she didn't want Makenzie to cry or anything, not on the day she was leaving to go back to Pennsylvania without her.

"My mom said that I have to stay here." Makenzie was telling Faith in the same way that Faith imagined Makenzie's mom must have told her, emphasizing the "*have to*" and "*here*." Faith peered at Makenzie with a confused look, and held her palms upward as if she were holding an invisible plate asking Makenzie to pass her more information.

"I can't come back home anymore. My mom said that Pennsylvania is what made me this way and that all the people there are bad for me and if I want to *live* here then I have to *stay* here." Makenzie's voice didn't crack. She didn't have any tears coming down her cheek. But she looked like she wanted to cry. She looked like she was trying to choke something back.

"What does that mean? I'm bad? Grandma is bad? Everyone in Pennsylvania is bad? The governor, the mayor maybe, but that's a little crazy to say the entire state of Pennsylvania is evil. I mean, what the fuck, Makenzie?"

"I told her about the boy with the mohawk and she said he doesn't love me, that he was just using me, and that I can't see him anymore."

"Of course she doesn't understand you and him! But how could she say who loves you and who doesn't? *Everyone* loves you! And using you? Does she think that's all that men do? She doesn't even know . . ." Faith could not even start to put into words all the things Makenzie's mom didn't know.

". . . And I told her about throwing up." Makenzie looked down and away and Faith's eyes got huge. "Because, I want to get help. I want to go to a doctor and a psychologist. And she said that Pennsylvania is what made me like this. That everyone up there is the reason that I'm so unhealthy."

"Oh, Mazie . . . why'd you tell her that?" Faith shook her head and spoke softly.

"Because she's my mom, Fay. I moved here so I could finally have a relationship with my mom and I want to be able to talk to her about things." Makenzie was defensive, as if for the first time ever she and Faith were not on the same side.

"It's fine then, whatever. I'll just come down here more often." Faith didn't want to argue about it. She didn't want to think about the entire state of PA mourning the loss of Makenzie and having to tell all their friends that even though she promised she'd be back that now she wouldn't.

Makenzie let a single tear roll down her cheek and said, "No, Fay," before wiping it with the dish towel she was wringing. "You can't come down here as much either." Anger flared up inside Faith and when she looked at Makenzie she no longer tried to hide her emotions.

"Why?" Faith knew she shouldn't have asked, she should have just left it at the population of Pennsylvania is bad.

"Mom said if you're down here every weekend then I'll never make new friends."

"What? Yes you will, you already made new friends! And we can hang out with them when I come down next. I'm sure I'll love them . . . why can't we all be friends? Why does it have to be one or the other?" Faith hated that they were even arguing about seeing each other when they had spent almost every weekend of their lives having sleepovers together at their Grandma's house. But Makenzie's mom wouldn't know about any of that. Because she was a state away and divorced from everything in Pennsylvania.

"Because. My mom said, it's unhealthy." Makenzie spoke soft and slow and Faith still couldn't understand. Faith didn't believe that Makenzie agreed with those words even as they were coming out of her mouth.

"What . . . like we'd be living a double life or something if we are here and there? It's not that hard. Doesn't your mom know that we've been through much worse? That this is easy now?" Faith could only hope it was something that simple.

"No . . . she means you and me. It's not healthy how much we need each other she said." Makenzie looked away right after she said it and folded up the wet dish towel to hang back on the stove.

"Makenzie. I've never been healthy." There were so many things wrong with what her aunt said: "*it's not healthy*" echoed in Faith's head. Faith didn't even know what to start defending first. She tried to look away. Her eyes moved back to the family room and suddenly she hated every picture in every frame on the walls because it was those frames that would hold Makenzie and not her. She looked back at Makenzie and choked back the screaming cry that she really wanted to let out. Instead she let her voice trickle out words, trying carefully just to sprinkle them out and not scream, "Did you tell her . . . did you tell her that we just love each other that much, that we've always been there . . ."

"Yeah . . . I told her . . . it doesn't matter." Makenzie sounded exhausted, like she had already lost this exact battle in a previous conversation. "I've got to do the laundry now . . ." Makenzie grabbed the dish towel from the stove and left.

Faith looked down at the placemat in front of her and hated it. She hated everything in that house as of two seconds ago. Because now, everything, every wall, every angle of that house was jumping right out and stabbing her. Faith didn't know how to defend a love so strong that it had saved them both time and time again. How to explain to someone that when you say *you will always be there* for someone that you can't just fucking accept someone else telling you to quit it.

Faith knew that Makenzie's mom didn't have any idea of the things that happened in Pennsylvania, because she wasn't there. She may have given birth to Makenzie, but she wasn't there any of the times that Makenzie came alive.

Makenzie's mom wasn't the one that talked Makenzie out of losing her virginity just because all her friends were doing it. Her mom wasn't the one who told her that the most important thing would be finding someone special one day that she cared about and who cared about her, and not just giving it up like all her stupid friends in school were doing. Her mom wasn't the one who taught her that her friends were doing nothing but giving up their childhood and that someday she would love someone enough that it wouldn't even feel like giving it away. It would feel right, like they were always meant to have a part of each other.

Makenzie's mom wasn't around when Makenzie wondered what she wanted to be when she grew up, when she tossed around ideas and dreamed of the future. She wasn't there to hear about how she wanted to be famous, and have a talk show and help people. And her mom wasn't the one who told her that she could do anything she wanted to, and that she'd be great at it.

Her mom wasn't the one constantly building her back up when the whole world broke her down. Her mom didn't help her with algebra homework. Her mom didn't call Makenzie up on a Monday just to see how school was, and to ask her how she did on her math tests.

Her mom wasn't even there when Makenzie tried on her first prom dress.

It was red.

And she looked fabulous.

Her mom wasn't the one who drove Makenzie to a deserted bank parking lot on a Sunday so that she could practice doing what every other teenager her age already knew how to do. And her mom didn't see the smile on Makenzie's face when she put the car into drive for the first time and slowly went in a circle. She wasn't there to hear Makenzie squeal with laughter as she tested the brakes and let go of the steering wheel to clap at herself.

Makenzie's mom wasn't there when life became a fight and survival became an instinct.

She wasn't there.

She wasn't there for any of it.

And to insinuate that the person Makenzie became was a mistake brought-to-you-by-the-state-of-Pennsylvania, was like saying she didn't know Makenzie at all.

And how could she say that their love for each other and their family was unhealthy? It was like saying she didn't know what love was—at all.

The exact amount of anger that Faith had had only moments ago, now softened into sadness.

Faith felt bad for Makenzie's mom.

She felt bad about everything.

You've got to trust yourself. Be gentle with yourself. And listen to yourself.

You're the only person who can get you through this now.

You're the only one who can survive your story, the only one who can write your future.

> *All you've got to do, when you're ready, is stand up,*
> *{and begin again.}*

. . . .

There's a break in the people coming up to me, I plead with my legs to try to walk and to just carry me up to the casket in the front of the room. I feel dizzy. Every step up to the casket feels like I am ripping my legs from the floor, like Velcro. I step up beside her closed casket, and I run my hand along the sides and I look at the container that she is encased in. I'm glad that I will never have to know what her face looks like without life. I'm glad that at least with the casket closed, part of me can pretend that maybe she really isn't in here. But as I run my hand over the details on the side of the casket, I can feel her. And I feel like I can't move back to my seat. Now that I'm up here, I feel like I can't leave her side.

Death is magnetizing.

My legs are stuck and I can only shrink my legs down like an accordion to keep from falling over. I'm bent over, and the shear fact that I can't move from the casket back to my chair, feeling like I can't go on again without her, brings me to tears. I'm hunched over my legs, my heels the only things standing, as I cry. I can hear whispers behind me, all panicked for me. Whispers all around for someone to come up to get me, like I'm drunk in the rain.

A soft hand guides me back to the wooden chair with cream upholstery. Carved wooden back chairs with white fabric try so hard to fill the viewing room and make it a little brighter, but it isn't enough. There's a staleness in the air that reveals this room has only ever been filled with tears and goodbyes.

Every breath is recycled air from someone else's loss.

I sit down, I hold on to a hand, and I brace myself with the other for the entrance of the hired Pastor. And I wonder what he could really say about her without knowing her. This rent-a-pastor commands the attention of the room and I just shake my head.

He talks about God and Death and I just wish we could talk about her life. I know he means well, and that he's talking about Heaven in the way that he was taught and approved to do so, but he's talking about sins and salvation and those words have a pain and judgment to them that I don't want to feel right now. And then, right as he's talking about her and her everlasting relationship with God and Jesus and the great beyond, right as he's fucking telling us that he is absolutely sure that she is indeed in the palm of God and that he has checked her into the nicest hotel in the sky, the Pastor calls her by the wrong name. Twice.

And I don't know if I heard him right, I'm only half paying attention and I don't know most of the biblical names he's referencing, but a lady, her aunt from her dad's side that I never met, stands up in front and corrects him. She sits back down and mumbles with a tissue, "Jesus wept."

He apologizes. But it means just about the same as everyone else in this room apologizing for my loss.

It doesn't matter.

She's gone.

Even the most sincere apologies mean nothing.

I watch him open his Bible and read, and I watch him close it and preach in front of the idle casket and I'm not even paying attention to the sentences he's selling to us, instead I'm thinking about how scared I am for what comes next.

I didn't think about anything past this funeral.

I didn't think about having to leave her, again.

The Pastor asks for anyone who would like to say a few words to come up to the center of the room, and the lady who corrected him stands up and tells a story about a time when my best friend was still alive and it makes me wish that I myself remembered being alive. It makes me feel like I am in her story with her, living again, if only in a memory.

And every part of my soul now aches, and my heart starts to stammer.

I turn to the girl with the dimples next to me. She hasn't smiled in days, but I can still see her dimples when she frowns. She's holding my left hand and I ask her desperately, "What time is it?" She turns to me and pats the top of my hand with hers and says, "I'm sorry, hun, it'll be over soon." She looks filled with pain, but without wanting to show it all, and her eyes tell me that if she could, she would walk right up to the center of the room and start ushering people out so that it would all just be over already.

227

But I nearly freak out.

"No . . . no . . . no . . . I don't . . . I don't want it to be over, I just want to stay longer in here with everybody . . . and . . ." And just as her casket came into the room closed, I can feel the end of this memorial service closing over me right now. Ending this. And I feel like I can't breathe.

She squeezes my hand and gives me an apologetic look.

And I squeeze back against her hand, hoping she won't let go.

The Pastor moves back to the center of the floor and he is the only one up there now. He asks if anyone, at all, would like to say anything else about her before we move to the burial.

And the room is silent.

He asks again, "Anyone . . . ?" and he holds his Bible like a football, just waiting to call the final play and usher us out to the field of the cemetery. The room is still. There are three hundred people sitting behind me and I can feel all of them cowering away from the question. I can feel them shrinking down and averting eye contact. The Pastor looks around and can hold the floor no longer, so he continues, "okay well, then I guess we will . . ."

"Wait," I mumble, and I find my voice, "Wait." I hold up my hand to cut him off. I motion to him that this isn't over. This can't be over yet. We can't just bury her. Not like this. I give the girl with the dimples her hand back.

And I stand.

I stand up, and because everyone is still sitting around me I feel tall. Because everyone else has cowered away from the question, I feel strong. They are stuck to their seats and I stand with my shoulders back. I walk with my black heels under my black pants under my black jacket and within three steps I'm in the center of the floor, in the front of the room. I'm face to face with her closed casket and I'm standing beside her. All I can think about is how she's lying down inside the casket and I've got to stand for her.

For the rest of my life, I will stand up for hers.

I take a deep breath and I turn around to see only black clothing and white eyes staring back at me.

And silence.

Everyone is silent.

Seats are all filled to the doorway and people are standing in the back of the room in rows like a Christmas Eve service at any church. I scan the crowd and I shake my head. I can't stop shaking my head. I shake my head at the empty seat that I rose up from, because every empty seat from now on will only ever remind me of her not being here.

I take a deep breath. But I'm breathing fine. I'm not shaking. I'm not choking on sobs or shoving tissues into my eyes. I should be quivering like I was in AP English when I had to give a speech in front of thirty people. But now, without a speech planned, and in front of three hundred people, I am not anxious at all. I should be choked up and I should be crying just saying her name standing this close to her lifeless body right now in front of so many people, but I'm not.

I'm just pissed.

I'm disappointed in more than just her being gone. I'm disappointed that of all the stories there are to tell about her, of all the things there are to say right now, no one wants to say anything but 'sorry.'

And I shake my head back and forth, "Really? No one can say anything about her? Well I'll tell you about her. She was great. She was full of love. She was so full of love that I can still feel it now. She didn't have room in her heart for hate, she hated school sometimes, but she didn't hate people, she had no time for that. And that's more than a lot of people can say for themselves . . ."

And I pause, looking around the room well knowing that there are people who actually have the audacity to be hating someone this very second, even in the middle of a funeral. And they are so busy hating others that they don't even know themselves well enough to know that the things they hate in other people exist in themselves too.

Hate is only a form of hypocrisy.

And she loved herself enough to not hate other people.

". . . And she was so full of life. She may have been young, but she lived. She lived more in her years than most people do their whole lives. She laughed . . . she had the best laugh . . ." My legs below me are holding me straight, strong, and tall, and I can only imagine that I am drawing this strength from her. There's no other answer for how I came upon it.

The same casket that weakened my knees to collapse below me just minutes ago is now behind me, providing strength. Just like the four days I've already unwillingly lived without her that are also behind me now. All of these painful things behind me are pushing me forward. Pushing me to stand tall.

And I continue to tell them stories about her, ". . . We grew up together and we did everything together. She was my best friend and my biggest fan, and I was hers. I looked up to her, but I also tried to teach her things. But most of the time, we just flew by the seat of our pants . . . and it was the best ride of my life. She had this ability to turn even the worst situations around. She smiled through pain, and if she were here she wouldn't want anyone to be crying. She wouldn't want me to cry . . . but when I cry, I'm not crying for her. I'm not crying for me, even. I'm crying for every single person in this world who will never get to meet her. Because she was great. She was my hero . . ."

And I pause. I pause long enough to get my mind from tangent to tangent without letting any tears, or snot, or pain drip out of me. And I tell them some more about her.

"She was the best, because she had no regrets . . ." And I look around the room and I wonder if the people crammed into this room even know what that means, so I explain it the best I can. I explain it the way that she used to explain things to me—with love. And when I'm done, I pause. And my legs won't allow me to leave the front of this room. My heart won't allow me to say "that's all" and sit back down. And so I think of another story to tell the three hundred people that are staring at me, right now. I look around at them, silently, all of the faces that are pieces and places from her life, and I look at them for inspiration and tell another story about her.

I'm not worried about running out of things to say, and for once I'm not even worried about breaking down in tears. I'm holding this room in place and I'm not even afraid of anyone ushering me off this impromptu stage, because everyone is just looking at me and eagerly waiting. Maybe if I were crying someone would come up and shoo me along, but I'm not crying. I've got words to say and my body knows that they can't come out if I'm crying.

And standing here, somehow I'm able to stretch a smile as I talk about her. And I know it's because I'm talking about love.

And I know that I've got to stand here, and get it all out.

I've got to tell her story.

Makenzie

Makenzie sat on her bed at her mom's house, next to the dresser they had bought at Ikea. Her room was decorated in all of the things that she loved, but it still didn't feel like her room. Her throat felt tight like tears were coming, and she tried to clear it, but instead a burp came up. A little gust of air from her belly that let her know that everything could be emptied right now if she wanted it to be.

She looked at photographs and notes in her lap from all of her friends and family back home that she missed so much. She hated being so far away from everybody that she loved. She hated that she could only sit in her room at night, alone, and think about everything that she missed knowing that none of those people in the photographs right then were in their room, alone, crying over her.

Because they all still had each other.

Still.

And she felt the weight of guilt in her stomach as she looked at the people in the photographs. Because they didn't know yet, that even though she promised, she wouldn't be coming back.

Her mom said that Faith could still visit at family events, holiday-type things and that the visits that they already had scheduled would be okay. But it was clear now to Makenzie that her mom would never approve of any of her life in Pennsylvania and that her past would follow her around like a constant reminder of her mother's distaste.

Makenzie knew that as long as she was still connected to anything in Pennsylvania, that her mom could never be really proud of her. Not the way Makenzie needed her to be. All she ever wanted was to make somebody proud.

Makenzie just never thought that she had to pick between family and friends, or her mom and her dad. But she did. By choosing to move with her mom, she chose to follow her mom's rules. She just never thought that one of those rules would be to cut her off from everything that she once loved. Every piece of life that made her who she was. She felt so stupid. So naive for thinking that she could have for once in her life gained something without losing.

But she couldn't.

And she should have known.

Because that would have been too easy.

Makenzie felt something in her stomach that reminded her of abandonment and she reached for her notebook on her nightstand.

"Hey Best Friend,

It's funny how I'm writing you a letter now since by the time I mail it and you'll get it we will have talked several times on the phone, computer, and through our star of course (lol) but I miss you. I miss everything. I've been thinking a lot about love. It hurts. Like a shit ton. Why does it have to hurt so much to love people? And I'm talking about all love, but I think there are only two kinds of love. One kind is when you just instantly love someone because they are innocent like babies or family, but then there's this other kind of love that's different it's like you meet someone and it grows and it's confusing because soon enough it feels like it's always been there with that one person, but you have to remind yourself that it wasn't always there. And that's the magic and the mystery of how painful this love is. Because it could go away and fade just as quickly as it grew. It's a painful, questionable, and unpromising thing. And it's scary. Because I don't want to lose it, but now before I'll ever get to tell him how much I love him and before it grows anymore, I've got to say goodbye . . . "

Makenzie dumped her head into her hands as she thought about dumping everyone in Pennsylvania. She thought about the boy with the mohawk and wondered how she could ever say goodbye to him, when she knew that her hands still fit inside his.

She hated that her mom thought she was too young to be in love. How could she be too young to love, but not too young to divorce everyone and everything in her life?

She understood that her mom just wanted her to have a fresh start. Makenzie wanted a fresh start too, but she didn't want to just completely bury the person she was a few months ago. She couldn't just re-boot her life and start over pretending that these relationships she held so close didn't exist or that they weren't worth keeping.

She couldn't just break up with her old life, move a state away, and consider it a new life like her mom did with her own divorce.

Makenzie never wanted that divorce, and she didn't want to go through another one. She just wanted to be happy. She just wanted to be somewhere in a house that felt like a home. She never thought that by wanting that one thing that she would have to slowly lose everything else that she loved.

She never wanted to have to say goodbye.

To anyone.

But now she had to do just that. And so now, she would have to plan a way on her next trip up to Pennsylvania, to see everyone she loved. And she would have to find a way to somehow say goodbye to them all.

She sat on her bed, and she looked at the clock.

11:05.

And Makenzie grabbed her charcoal pencils and sketch pad, and waited for a wish.

Faith

Another trip to the Hospital and another world of questions.

Faith was sick and tired of being sick and tired.

She sat up on her bed, thankful that she was at least at home and not stuck to a hospital bed. And she held her hand over her heart, trying hard to slow the beats and pain that every rush of blood pushed into her chest. She tried not to think about what the doctors meant that morning when they said that the infection was in the sac lining her heart and how much better that was than if the infection had been inside of her heart.

She tried not to think about what would happen if the infection and inflammation spread. She tried not to think about what caused it. And she tried not to think about her entire body attacking itself, but that's what it did best.

She called Makenzie for a distraction.

"Faith!" Makenzie answered the phone.

"Hey, how's school going?" Faith didn't want to worry Makenzie with her latest hospital news. Besides, it couldn't really be considered news if Faith was always sick.

"Eh, okay, it's alright I guess . . ." Makenzie sighed.

"Just okay, huh?" Faith asked in shallow short breaths. Even a medium size breath would expand her lungs to push on the inflammation around her heart, sending pain up her entire chest into her jaw.

"It just sucks, Fay. I mean my mom's family is great down here and I love my little sisters and am making new friends and everything, but like . . . for real . . . it just fucking sucks. I miss everyone. I miss my old life. I miss staying out late and just looking at the stars. I miss corn muffins at 3 am. I miss Grandma's mashed potatoes. I even miss sitting through an hour of church every Sunday with Grandpa . . ."

"But you've got your mom now, right? That's good?" Faith tried to sound cheerful.

"I just didn't think I had to give up everything else. I didn't . . ." Makenzie stopped to think and Faith interrupted,

"I guess that's what they mean when they say you can't have your cake and eat it too . . . huh?" Faith tried to use a cliché to make Makenzie laugh. But it wasn't funny. And right after she said that she cringed knowing she shouldn't have brought up food. Especially not something as big as a whole cake. The moment of silence on the other end of the line made Faith panic and try to think of something else to quickly fill the dead air.

"That's such a bullshit saying, Faith. Why the fuck would someone have cake if they weren't going to eat it too? What's the point then? No one just buys cake to look at it and watch the icing melt to mold. Having cake is *eating* cake. You buy cake to eat it. That's the whole point. That saying should be like "*you can't have your cake and eat someone else's too.*" But I am only trying to eat *my* cake and it's not even a big piece it's like the smallest freaking cupcake ever but life won't let me eat it. Instead life just keeps taking a bite out of me and it's got a big chunk of my left ass cheek in its mouth right now and it's not pretty . . ." Makenzie took a deep breath.

"I'm sorry, Makenzie." Faith knew how much it sucked. But she didn't know what else to say. Her inflamed heart sank at the thought of Makenzie getting off the phone thinking about life as if it were cake and purging all of the feelings in the way that she always did. So Faith changed the subject, "I'm sorry, I love you, how was your doctor's appointment?" Faith tried hard not to just spill every scary detail of her own doctor's appointment because she knew that Makenzie would only worry. And she didn't want her to worry or stress any more than she already was. She didn't want to add anything that would aggravate the bulimia or make her mad at doctors especially after Makenzie was so excited about her own doctor's appointment.

"Well, it was okay, he gave me a prescription of something that will help with the acid reflux." Makenzie sounded annoyed.

"Oh that's good, that's what you wanted right, something to help the acid so it doesn't burn so much?" Faith nodded her head through the phone line.

"Yeah. But . . ." Makenzie sounded disgusted.

"What does it have weird side effects or something?" Faith knew all too well to find out the side effects of the medicines first.

"No it's not that, it's not the medicine, that's great and everything, I just wanted him to help more I guess. When I told him about throwing up, I told him the truth, and he just basically said not to do that and what would happen if I kept doing it. He told me about how I could lose my period, and lose my teeth or have a heart attack. And I already lost my period. Now I'm worried about losing everything else. It's just . . . I can't stop. I can't. That's why I need help, I want to know how to stop. I already know that it's bad. And now knowing how much worse it is . . . I'm just . . . now I'm even more scared. I just wish I could go somewhere and talk to a psychologist or a therapist or something . . ." Makenzie's voice sounded wounded.

Faith felt all the pain of loving someone from the outside while they fought a silent battle alone on the inside. She felt so helpless. She didn't know what to say now. Sometimes confusion is just wanting so badly to not say the wrong thing. She was just as scared as Makenzie. But she knew if she said too much that it could trigger the bulimia; too many questions, making Makenzie only worry more, would lead to a bad night. Faith wanted to say a million things. She wanted to tell Makenzie how much she hated that stupid disease and what it did to her. And how much less she thought of the people in Makenzie's life that made that disease worse, the ones that made it come alive. Faith wished she could have told her that she hated the way Makenzie still loved the people that triggered her bulimia, that she wished instead of loving herself less that Makenzie could have just loved those people less. But she knew that wasn't how the disease worked.

So she tried to sound hopeful for her best friend, ". . . I'm sorry, Mazie. Can your mom find you a good therapist and you can . . ." Faith tried to add hope, she knew how disappointed it could be after meeting with any doctor. They never say anything to make anyone feel better.

"It's fine, Fay. I'm fine." To try to put an end to her disappointment, Makenzie abruptly ended the conversation.

But Faith knew that nothing was fine.

Nothing was ever just *"fine."*

No matter how hard she pretended it was.

Makenzie

She had just gone for a run, and she thought that exercising would be enough for her disease or enough to at least distract the disease. But it wasn't. So after drinking a bottle of water after her run, she needed to get rid of it.

Even the water was too much now.

And she'd try to convince herself that it was just water, and her body needed it, but her body wouldn't let her forget that it wasn't about the food. It was the feelings. And as soon as the cold water hit the fires of her gut, it wasn't welcomed there. Her body began responding almost immediately with a rapid heartbeat, her stomach moving in and out, almost gagging, while Makenzie wasn't even anywhere near a toilet. She was still in the kitchen and couldn't make it to the bathroom. She looked around quickly and leaned over the kitchen sink. Clear water spilled out of her. Her body was now controlling the heaving.

She hated the bulimia. She hated that she was becoming a hostage to it. She hated that it was more out of control than she thought it could ever get.

And she hated that her mom blamed Pennsylvania for all of this happening. She hated herself for letting it happen. But most of all she hated that people thought that understanding bulimia would mean that they condoned it. Like the ounce of compassion she needed now could only be given if they approved of what she did.

She hated that people thought like that. And what they didn't get was that by withholding compassion, they were only giving the bulimia more control. That it was more fucked up than anyone would ever realize. Because it wasn't taking sides of right and wrong. It was a fight now. It was a constant fight and she wasn't going to win without help.

Home is not so much a place, as it is a feeling . . .
. . . Or sometimes, a person.

You will get to feel at home again one day.
Heaven will wait for you.

. . . .

The Pastor at the head of the room, still holding the Bible, gives instructions of what we are all to do next and where we are to go. There are people here from Pennsylvania, Maryland, Florida, New York, North Carolina, New Jersey, and Hawaii, and so he explains slowly how we are to get there and where to park, like a teacher to a classroom of children about to take a field trip.

The worst field trip ever.

And I panic. Because I don't have my field trip buddy.

I lost my buddy.

And I start to feel like the child that I really am.

I am forever lost without her.

People start to file out doorways, and I can't breathe. The feeling of all three hundred people in the Funeral Home leaving at once closes in on me.

Death is repeated abandonment.

And as people funnel out to the parking lot and branch off into pods of conversations, I move to the back of the room, so that I can't see the people leaving out through the heavy doors. I don't know what I'm doing but I just know that I can't leave yet.

I see our boys, in suits, circled in conversation near the back of the room as if they were all hanging out at a high school football game and not at a funeral. As I get closer to them I can see that they aren't really talking at all, their heads are hung and their feet are nervous. And when they look up at me coming, I can see that all of their eyes are holding in tears that I'm sure will come out in the form of screams or punches later, much later, when they are each alone.

The boy with the mohawk steps towards me, reaching for me. Most people only see what's in front of them, and even then they will only pick and choose what they really want to see, but the boy with the mohawk sees more than what's in front of him, he sees what's not there too. He knows me well enough to see all that's missing and he wraps his arms around my waist in a hug that feels like for just a second that I'm not as broken as I really feel. I wish that it were true, and I tighten my fists and squeeze my arms tighter around his neck hoping that if I squeeze him hard enough that he could be the glue that holds me together. My eyes are shut hard, making the familiar smell of his cologne stronger and in my head I can't stop begging, *"Please don't let go, please don't let go, please don't let go."* But I know that we have to eventually let go.

I'm learning that now.

It's just so hard to do.

And just before the hug ends, he squeezes me a little tighter. Then with his arms on my shoulders, he pulls me outward in front of him to look at me. Looking at him now brings so much emotion to the surface and some of the things I wish I could say to him leak out of my eyes. He brings his hand up, with his thumb out, and wipes a tear falling from my cheek.

And for a moment, we have a moment.

Just a moment though . . .

Death is forever interrupting life.

An older man, someone who works for the Funeral Home, breaks into our circle and asks for the pallbearers to follow him. When he sees me he locks eyes and he whispers to ask if I would like to see the casket one last time before everyone lines up and carries it out, but I do not understand the question. The way he asked me made it sound like a sad privilege. I look around the circle and every single one of the boys is staring at me frozen with wide eyes, like the time last summer when I held a Black Cat firecracker in my hand and lit it, how they stared as I held my palm up, out away from my body while the red snake-like-mini-explosive hissed and sparked. Their eyes look the same now, wide open, scanning me and looking for signs of damage.

"I don't . . . know . . . ?" And my voice pleads for help.

"He means . . . do you want to see her . . . they're letting anyone who wants to see her . . . take a look . . . in the back." The boy with the goatee puts words in front of me, slowly, and I can tell that he's hoping that I don't make him say any more than he has to. But I don't get it. Does he mean see her . . . dead?

"If you want to see her they'll open the lid for you . . . if you want to, I'll walk back with you." The boy with the mohawk holds out his hand reassuringly, and I want to take it. But I don't know. And I look at all the boys. They are all still looking at me with big red eyes. And I look at the boy with the goatee sideways and he admits, ". . . We all went already."

And I lose my breath. Realizing that any faint spark of hope that I had by pretending she really wasn't inside that casket, was now lost.

She's really in there.
They saw it for themselves.
Quickly I look around and I ask them,
"How . . . how did she . . ."
And no matter how good she looked, I know that they can't tell me that she looked alive. So instead of answering, they all just look at me.

"Do you want to see her . . . ?" The boy with the mohawk asks me sympathetically. The older man has already walked away and time is running out. Everyone will be leaving again soon, and I have to decide this second if I want to see what she looks like inside that casket.

I'd give anything to see her again.
Anything.
But I don't want the last time I see her to be like this.
I don't know what to do.
And suddenly I'm asking myself if I will regret *not* seeing her dead. If I will regret *not* seeing her lifeless, colorless, emotionless body in front of me the one last chance that I had. And that's the kind of fucked-up shit that death will make you ask yourself. There's no right answer. But I have a million questions. Did they comb her hair to the right side? Does the dress we picked out look okay on her? Did they add any pink to her cheeks? Is she still wearing the same necklace that matches mine?

I look at the boys again. The boy with the baseball hat winces at the decision I have to make, and he slowly shakes his head. The boy with the goatee shrugs one shoulder and shakes his head. And the boy with the motorcycle leans in and tells me, "She's not . . . she looks okay . . . but it's not her." And he shakes his head before strongly urging, "Don't."

And now my eyes are wide.
I don't want to feel the way that he does.

I don't want to feel like I lost her again. I know I'll have to lose her a hundred more times in different ways before the day is over, but this time, this moment I can choose not to.

I shake my head.

"I'm okay."

And the boys all nod their heads, and the man that works at the Funeral Home motions them over to learn their part. To give them directions on how to walk someone to their grave. I watch the boys walk away, wishing that at least one of them could come with me and hold my hand instead of that casket.

But they can't.

No one can hold my hand forever.

So I clasp my own hands together in front of myself.

Through the doorway of the next room I can see someone familiar. It's her dad. Even from far away, I can see exactly where he is standing because there is no one around him. In this moment there is no one coming up to him and basting him in apologies. He looks around the room like he's looking for someone, but I know he's only looking around for who he's wishing he could look for.

But she's already here.

And even she is about to leave us again.

I look at him across the room, and I think about how hard it must be for him to stand in this place right now. To try to be someone that he doesn't want to be. A father to a dead girl. I feel bad for him in a way that I don't feel bad for anyone else, because I have sympathy for him that isn't about her death. And I think about how I could possibly ever tell him that I'm sorry without it sounding like a cliché. I try to think about how I could make my voice project what I am most sorry for: their time lost.

I start to walk over to him, dodging eye contact with anyone who might stop me and slow my courage on my way to talk to him.

I approach him, taking up the empty space in front of him. He says "Hi," nervously, and he does something that looks like a shameful smile. I wonder if he's thinking of the last time that he saw her or if he's only thinking about the times that he didn't see her. And I say "Hi," back and I try to smile too. I feel like my mouth is only open and wide and that my lips aren't stretching to curve around my teeth in a smile but that instead I might look like I'm going to bite him. But I'm not, I'm not going to chew him out like I'm sure other people in this room are waiting to do. I can only feel bad for him. I feel bad for him because I know that she didn't hate him.

I know that.

{But he doesn't.}

And so I try to think of a way to tell him that she didn't hate him. That even when she should have, even when she tried to, she just couldn't hate him. But I can't find the words to say these things to him, because in my mind, all I can think about, while trying to push out these feelings, is how she should be the one here standing in front of him now, and not me.

She should be here now.

But she's not.

And even though I know she wouldn't mind me speaking on her behalf now or ever, I just can't find the words.

I can't stop thinking about how much she deserved to see him again. Standing next to him now, I'm just filling up with pain.

A part of me just can't stop hurting for her past.

And the other part can't stop hurting for her dad's future.

Makenzie

She had driven up to Pennsylvania in record time. She even stopped to get flowers not only for Faith's Graduation that day, but it was Faith's birthday too. She bought her the prettiest flowers she could find, but they still weren't pretty enough. This would be her only visit to Pennsylvania in June, and she wanted to make the best of it.

Makenzie insisted on driving Faith everywhere that day. It was her liberation, she had just gotten her license and had to play chauffer to show everyone her car. Her mom and stepdad had let her drive their Mazda 626. It was no black Jetta, but it was black and it was perfect in the fact that it had four wheels and was in good condition.

They drove to the boy with the goatee's house where all of their friends were getting ready. Makenzie was so excited for everyone, it may as well have been her Graduation Day too, even though she'd have to wait another year.

Makenzie saved Faith's cards for when the girls were inside the house, sitting in the living room. Makenzie pulled out handmade birthday and graduation cards. One had a birthday cake with an 18 on the front and the other had blue and black hand lettering with the word *Congratulations* going diagonally across the card. Faith read each one and thanked Makenzie with a hug, "You're such a nerd, you don't have to make me cards, but I love them thank you."

"Yes I do, I will always make you cards!" Makenzie sat and pulled at her skirt, "Also, I love this skirt, thank you—it's so perfect." Makenzie was wearing a dark brown stretch fabric pencil skirt with light brown and red abstract roses on it that matched her red top. Her heels made the outfit even dressier. She looked so grown up, but not as grown up as Faith in her white dress pants to match her white gown.

"I knew you'd like that skirt, and it does look good on you." Faith complimented her own buying decision as Makenzie stood up to walk herself to a mirror and turned around like a model.

"The best thing about it, is that it makes my butt look good." Makenzie stood with her hands on her hips, showing off her ulterior motive for wearing the outfit other than the fact that Faith had given it to her. She was bound to run into the boy with the mohawk later that day and she wanted everything to look its best, especially her butt. If she had to let him go and be walking away from him she had to at least make sure the she looked good doing it.

She sat back down and looked at Faith in admiration, "So, are you ready for this . . . ?" Makenzie had a huge smile.

"Yeah, I guess, I mean it's no big deal really. It's just high school graduation." Faith flattened out the front of her white gown as the boy with the goatee's mom helped all of the boys knot their ties, and she teased them about how the next time they might all be this dressed up would be when they each got married. The boys squirmed away from their ties at the thought of marriage.

Makenzie giggled at the thought of everyone getting married someday.

"It's a huge deal Fay! This is the beginning of the rest of your life here. You're going to be going to college and getting a job, and before you know it we're going to be getting married and having little babies!" Makenzie hoped that Faith didn't fight the fact that she put "going to college" in that list.

"I know." Faith said calmly as if Makenzie had just reminded her of the time and not the future.

"You know, Fay . . ." Makenzie scootched closer right across from Faith, all of her energy centered on her open hands in her lap. "I was going to wait to tell you this, but I've already decided that whenever I have kids, when I have a little girl, I'm going to name her after you. And I don't care who I am with, if they don't like that name too bad, because she's going to be named 'Faith'." Makenzie had just exploded her plan, she couldn't keep it a surprise until she actually did have kids. She just wanted Faith to know in that moment how proud of her she was and how proud she always would be.

Faith smiled, "Mazie! That's ridiculous. What if I have a kid and I name her after you first, then our kids will be calling their aunts by the same name haha they will just be little versions of us but in a really odd way . . ." Faith giggled thinking about it.

"Really though," Makenzie tried to be serious, "You're my hero, Fay." Makenzie got tears in her eyes and could see the same in Faith's.

"Mazie . . ." Faith showed emotion for the first time that day.

"It's true . . ." Makenzie leaned over and hugged her.

Faith

After Graduation, the yearly birthday anthem was sung by Faith's mom and Makenzie. Faith stood through the long chorus of Happy Birthday and thought about what one wish she needed more than anything to come true. "Fay! Close your eyes and make a wish, babe!" Makenzie held the cake, the candles creating sparkles in her eyes.

Faith closed her eyes.

She enunciated the wish in her head as if it mattered how clear she was about it.

She repeated it three times in her head for good luck.

And she blew out eighteen candles in one single breath.

Faith's mom and Makenzie clapped and Faith shrugged her shoulders with a smile.

She didn't want any cake, only the wish.

"Fay, you know I would stay longer right, but . . ." Makenzie put the lighter that she used for the candles back into her purse. Faith's mom was cutting cake and handing out pieces to the girls as if there was an imaginary line behind them of people forming, and she wanted to make sure that the girls got a piece.

"I know," Faith nodded the kind of nod that goes only down and reached to give Makenzie a hug. Faith knew it would have been hard enough for Makenzie to say "Hi" to everyone she wanted to see in one day trip, without having to find people to say "Goodbye" to.

"I have to see him, Fay. You know I have to say goodbye. I have to see him one last time." Makenzie pulled away from the hug to make sure that Faith understood and that her feelings weren't hurt.

Makenzie looked into Faith's eyes with tears in her own, but Faith just smiled, "You'll find him, Makenzie." Like she knew some kind of secret of the universe that Makenzie didn't know yet. And Faith nodded again, "You'll find him, don't worry!" Faith looked into Makenzie eyes and could see the reflection of a happy tear coming.

"Fay! Did you . . ." Makenzie shook her head.

"I can't tell you what I wished for, or you know it won't come true then, silly! Now go find him." Makenzie hugged Faith hard like it was the last time she would ever see her, and Faith wrapped her arms around Makenzie too easily. It was the thinnest Makenzie had ever been. Faith looked over Makenzie's shoulder at the one bite that Makenzie had taken out of her cake and wished that they could have had more time to talk.

She wished that everything didn't have to always be so rushed.

But she was an official graduate now, and growing up meant that there wouldn't always be time for cake and that there were more things to say goodbye to than she knew.

"Just remember, goodbyes are overrated." Faith thought of her non-existent goodbye from her dad, and reminded Makenzie with one look that she was proof that it's possible to still be breathing without a goodbye.

Still.

But Faith knew Makenzie well enough to know that Makenzie had probably practiced this goodbye to the boy with the mohawk as much as she practiced their first hello, and she knew that Makenzie would find him. She knew that she would find him, because she knew that wishes, when they were self-less and for other people, almost always came true.

And Faith watched Makenzie go out the door to find the boy with the mohawk.

The air is different now.
You've never been more aware of all the air around you.

Even the tiniest hairs on your arm will spread from your skin to reach this air, because even they are more aware of it now, they can feel it.

Heaven is all around you.

. . . .

Driving to the cemetery from the service, cars with little magnetic flags create a parade following behind her. The girl with the cross around her neck sits in the passenger seat next to me as I drive, and we talk about Heaven.

There are so many new things I feel now that I've never felt before. And one of them is her. Even though she is completely wiped from this reality I can still feel her.

Still.

The sky is blue with puffy clouds and the sun is everywhere, reflecting off cars' windshields as they are stopped at intersections waiting for our living-death-parade to go by. And for a minute I try to pretend that all I see is really all that's there. I try to pretend that it's all sun and sky and the world is bright yellows and blues just like Grandma's kitchen, while inside I still feel like pouring rain. I wish it really was pouring rain and that we'd all be drowning in Heaven's tears right now. I wish that even windshield wiper blades could be swiping out groans of "this sucks, this sucks, this sucks." But Heaven's not crying today.

For some reason it's beautiful outside, and I already know that beautiful isn't just an adjective, it's only ever going to be a synonym for her.

The cars in the front of our parade are only traveling 20 mph, and the girl with the cross around her neck and I talk more about what we think Heaven is like. We both agree that it is superior in every way to this, to Earth. Cars on side streets wait at stop signs, standing still watching and waiting for our funeral train to pass.

I wonder if our impromptu hundred car parade is holding up their days. I wonder if her death is making other people who never knew her late, or angry. I hope that for the ten generous minutes they are stopped by death that they think about life.

I hope they appreciate the reminder. And I hope they take a minute to really look at the line of cars passing them, to see all of the beater cars and band decals on our bumpers, to hear our teenage music coming out of windows, and know that life is short. You only live once, but sometimes it can be much shorter.

Sometimes, 'you-only-live-half-a-once.'

I hang my left arm out the window and I let the wind push my hand up and down, making waves. I pull at the air with my palm and I think about the unlimited-ness of where she is. She is three cars in front of us, but she's also in the air that's running through my fingers. She's everywhere now, and I'm still trying to get used to that and learn how to honor that feeling.

There's this hope that this isn't the end. Not for her and not for me, even though it still feels like it is for both of us.

I think about seeing her again in Heaven, feeling her arms wrapped so tight around me and erupting with only joy and love. I think about how I'll feel her arms around me even before they are. I think about the air being filled with swirling colors. I think about everything having a rainbow radiance. I think about light all around and how light I will feel too. How one day, it will all just be love and light.

And I never realized that I had so many ideas about Heaven. Once she became a part of Heaven, I started to feel like Heaven was a part of me too. I can't explain the feeling of realizing that this world is just inside another world. Like playing with a dollhouse inside of a real house when we were little. I remember playing Barbies and dolls with her all the time when we were little, but I don't remember the day we stopped playing. It just kind of happened.

I'll remember this day though. I'll remember how I gave up the dollhouse of my old life. That smaller world I lived in was always inside this great big world, and I'll never live inside there again.

And although I never got to plan our next visit and ask her when we'd see each other again, I have to be okay with "Heaven" as the answer. Even though I'm not sure how to get there. I will wait for her to come get me. I will wait for her to wake me up one day from this life.

I feel as heavy as I've felt since this began, but the heaviness is different now. I feel all the heaviness of Heaven weighing on my shoulders with the responsibility to keep her memory alive. To take in the sun and let it burn up any despair inside me. To let in the night but only to remind me to shine like the shooting star that she is.

Because death cannot capture love.

It has stolen her breath, it has killed my dreams, but it cannot ever weaken the strength of our love because love is the only thing that can never die. If anything, it has only made it stronger. Because my love for her now reaches far beyond what it ever could before. It reaches beyond anything I knew before. My love for her isn't just across the plain of people on Earth, it's now spanning trees and clouds and into the entire universe until it reaches her, wherever she is.

It's everywhere.

We pull into the gated cemetery and follow cars slowly pulling up next to gravestones. We wait for just a minute in the parked car before getting out, as if there is anything left to prepare for . . . as if the air inside our car is easier to breathe than the air outside.

I get out of the car and see the pop-up tent that will host everyone's goodbye. There is green carpet over fresh dirt and chairs placed in a row against the edge of the tent. And there are flowers here, already. The way this is all set up proves the idea that the Funeral Home and the cemetery grounds workers really do hold events like this every day. Every day this happens. They are some of the few collections of people in this world prepared for death to happen, and they are prepared for it every day.

I stand in the grass with black high heels sinking into the soft earth, and I watch the boys pull her casket from the back of the hearse and carry it. With one arm each, they walk past veterans of the dead through aisles of tombstones to place her casket on top of metal bars under the tent over a deep hole.

Their faces reveal how heavy the casket is, although I doubt she weighed more than a hundred pounds. I think about the dress she's wearing inside as I look at the outer decorative gunmetal gray of the handles that clink softly against the metal of the casket as they move up and down.

People are gathering close, and I'm not sure where to stand, but I'm sure someone will tell me. There's a lady I don't recognize, looking at me like she wants to say something honorable or something awkward, I can't tell. She reaches her hand out to grab mine and says to me in a voice slightly above a whisper, "I just want you to know . . . that you . . . what you said back there, you saved the funeral."

And I'm not sure what to say to that.

I try to absorb her words and I wonder in the history of funerals if such a phrase has ever been thought, let alone said aloud.

I'm not sure it's possible to save a funeral. But for a minor moment in time I almost feel like something I did made a difference, that maybe something I said made people feel a little bit better. But the moment, like her life, is short lived, because I can't help but feel if our roles were reversed, if she were the one that was here now, that she would have known exactly what to say without pause and she would have said it better than I ever could have.

I should have said more.

And in my mind I realize I will.

The rest of my life will be a eulogy for her.

So I just say, "Thank you." And she smiles.

Someone comes to guide me to a seat. There are a handful of chairs they lead me to in front of the casket and somehow I've become some kind of princess in the royalty of death. And it feels like they are ushering me to the front row of my own funeral. I'm already too close to be any closer, but they sit me in the front anyways.

And the Pastor is ready with more prayers. He blesses the casket, he blesses the ground, and he blesses us. I can't help but feel like we need the prayers the most.

And then a car alarm goes off.

Loud enough to wake the living.

And everyone standing around is fumbling for keys to see if it's their car that's making a scene. A few small beeps from key fobs, and the car alarm is over.

But my panic is just beginning.

One more prayer, and just like that, everything is officially over. Just like that, people are leaving again.

And the leaving is what always hurts the most.

Backs are turned to her, and my heart breaks thinking about how everyone seems to be okay with it all just being over, how they're all just okay with leaving her here. I know there is nothing that they can do. I know that she is already gone. But part of her isn't.

And so I walk towards her.

I walk up next to the casket and lay six roses on top. I don't remember picking out these roses that I'm holding or paying for them, like the feeling of getting somewhere without remembering the drive. But I remember exactly what each rose represents, the meaning behind why I picked each one that I'm holding on to so tightly that I can feel the thorns. My bottom lip tenses at the thought of being on autopilot for the rest of my life, not knowing how I will get anywhere or do anything in the future with meaning, other than knowing the feeling at the end, like these roses, everything will be for her.

And I lay them down one by one, and in my head I tell her. And I honor the parts about her that I will miss most. A red rose for her passion for life. A white rose for the peace we always wanted, the peace that she has now. A bright pink rose for our friendship. A soft pink rose for love that never ends. A fiery orange with red tips for the fight that she had in her. And a peach rose for life everlasting.

As soon as I set the last rose down, I start to cry again.

Because I don't have anything else to give her.

I don't have anything else left.

And the boy with the motorcycle touches my arm and helps me off the green funeral carpet covering the uneven ground and guides me back, pulling me away from the casket. I know he's doing me some kind of favor, doing her a favor maybe by watching over me, but I don't want to leave her. I reach out my hand for the roses as he guides me away, and something about the way the roses lay limp over the body of the casket makes me sad about being alive. The roses are alive, for now, but they still aren't as beautiful as she.

They aren't enough. And the weakness that comes with knowing that, swallows me up for a moment.

We leave from under the pop-up canopy, and the sun is so incredibly bright. I guess no one told the sun that it should just stop shining.

But that's just it.

The world keeps turning effortlessly. The person who I love the most vanished without causing even a hiccup in the rest of the world.

And there's nothing I can do about it. That might be the thing that hurts the most right now. The only thing I can do is face it. And I look directly up to face the sun and the bright sky and with my eyes squinting I feel the sun's rays and they burn. It hurts so badly, because every ray of sunshine says that this happens a million times a day. A thousand times a second people are leaving.

And already I feel like I need to brace for someone else to leave next. How often will death take away life?

I don't know.

And that's what's scary.

And then, when my mind stretches beyond the pain of loss, I look back down at the people leaving this place now and I can see little kids running and falling down in the cemetery.

And I realize that people are coming too.

People are being born every minute and some of them are coming just as fast as those leaving.

Maybe the Earth is just rotating from gears of people coming and gears of people leaving like a revolving door of energy.

Maybe life coming in and death going out and the love for both is exactly what keeps the world turning . . .

Makenzie

She was driving away. She passed every car on the road and felt bad for them as if everyone that day was going to the same place and she was going to get there first. She didn't know where they were going. But she was going home.

The July sun was bright and the horizon was beckoning her.

The road was winding and she drove like the wheels were singing the exact song of her heart.

It sounded like freedom.

She just wanted to be free.

She thought about her Grandma, and about how in just minutes she would be walking into that house that held her life story. No one knew her better than the walls of that house and she just wanted to get there. She imagined how her Grandma and Grandpa would say *"Oh there's our little Kenzie,"* and how it would make her smile because she just wanted to be somebody's something. Grandma would no doubt offer her food, and Makenzie swore to herself in the car that whatever it was she would eat it and not even think about throwing up because she missed Grandma's food so much.

She would be better once she was home, she knew it.

She saw the big blue sign with the green keystone and white lettering ahead that said *Pennsylvania Welcomes You.*

She sped up.

Her heart raced so fast that her chest hurt.

She passed the sign.

And she felt relief.

She had made it home.

Faith

Faith had thought about skipping college entry testing a million times that week. She couldn't believe it was on the same morning that Makenzie was making a trip to Pennsylvania and she didn't want to miss a second with her. She hated missing her.

But she knew how much Makenzie wanted her to go to college and Faith agree to at least take the entry exams. She drove around the local community college campus looking for the right building. All of the buildings looked the same and none of them were labeled where she could see it.

She drove two laps around the campus and felt something in her stomach that reminded her of her disease. She felt like she could throw up, and then her stomach did what it always did, and she begged it not to.

Not now.

Just not now.

Please not now.

She parked her car and leaned into her stomach with her head on her steering wheel and closed her eyes. She tried to clear her head and think about flowers and clouds and anything peaceful. "*It's okay, it's okay, it's okay,*" she repeated to herself.

But it wasn't okay.

Nothing was okay. Her stomach was seizing in pain and her chest was tight. She felt like she could barely breathe. And so she put her car into drive and headed for the only place where she never felt as sick as she actually was.

She headed to her Grandma's house.

She held her stomach with one hand and her other hand, shaking, gripped the wheel. Her eyes blinked heavy, squinting with pain.

She thought about how that first hug would feel like home.

She just needed to be at home.

There isn't enough sympathy in the world to lift you up high enough to get over the grief.
Grief isn't a wall.
      You can't get over it.
         You can't go around it.
And it will only get worse if you try to hide from it.
      And time itself won't erase it.
      Grief is a part of healing that needs to be experienced.

      The only way you can start to feel free from never-ending sinking pain is to do the single most terrifying thing there is . . . you've got to face it.

. . . .

I drive past the black-gated entrance to the development and notice how the gates have shed dead paint chips from their arms, revealing age spots of rust underneath. I drive slowly over gravel and cringe at the sound tiny rocks make as they kick up behind me. They kick up and bounce off the metal of my car making my entrance seem so loud in such a quiet place.

I slowly turn the wheel of my car down a long driveway and I park in a familiar spot that I imagine parking in front of my first apartment might feel like someday.

I feel like I'm home, but it's lonely.

I step out of the car and I pull my things out with me. My purse, my notebook, the stuffed animal that the girl with the tattoos gave me a couple weeks ago. I grab my phone and a bag of obnoxiously bright yard ornament pinwheels, because I thought that they might make her happy.

Or maybe make me remember being happy.

I close the car door and the 2:00 pm summer sun highlights me as the only living soul here. I walk up to fresh dirt that's smoothed in the shape of a rectangle. I look around at the rows of concrete and marble sticking up around me, and can see they aren't in perfect rows and lines like they appeared to be as I drove up. Instead they are placed like checkers on a board, waiting for something to move into empty spaces. The fresh holes in the ground are scattered like stars in the sky and I know now that the line to Heaven isn't straight, it's zig-zagged.

I tiptoe over the prettiest grass and I walk to where she is and where I know she isn't.

The breeze is gentle but moving enough that I'm glad for the pinwheels. Maybe if I stick them in the ground and watch them turn in the breeze, I'll feel more like she's here. I know she's not really here in the ground, but I can't stop feeling like it's the closest to her that I can be, for now.

I unload my belongings in the grassy aisle of the cemetery, and I begin to outline the rectangle of soil with the shimmering metallic petaled pinwheels. Each has two colors, reflecting blues and greens and oranges and the silver petals in between reflect the sun.

I pick out one that is blue and silver and one that is red and silver and I place them into the dirt with intention like candles on a cake. Careful. With wishful thinking. Each one's bendable plastic white stick goes into the ground too easily, and it reminds me how fresh everything still is. I think for only a second about how the earth below me will be hard and full of weeds one day instead of soft and moveable. I shiver thinking of coming here as an adult. I weaken at the thought of ever growing up without her. The thought of years ahead where everything will change except her still being gone, makes me feel an emptiness flush through my body sending warmth to my legs.

I move my head shaking it just quickly enough to signal better thoughts to surface. And I quickly fast forward my mind to a time when the earth below will hold my body forever too.

And I feel relieved.

I'll get there too one day.

She'll wait for me.

I sit down beside the rectangle of fresh earth and I brush the dirt on my hands on to my jeans. I can't help but feel like I'm not clean enough. Not enough for Heaven. And the clouds above me all move in the direction of "No," telling me I'll have to wait. I plead with the grass around me, pulling at it and letting it go. But even the ripping sound of grass is telling me "No," I have to wait.

Pity sweeps over me, no longer for myself, but now for the grass beneath me and around me. Grass so untouched and unadmired, planted only for the illusion of life. For the addition of color in an otherwise gray and brown world.

To assure people that it's not all death.

But I'm positive that even the patches of grass around these gravesites are wishing that they could have been planted in the playground across the street. I look past the entrance of the cemetery, the gates weakened by age but still strong enough to separate the living from the dead, and I see swings moving up and down. And now that I see them I can hear the faint giggles of children.

I look back at the pinwheels beside me, and they are all still.

For a moment I wish that I could be in that playground too.

I wish I were swinging in the air making wind around me rather than sitting here waiting for the wind to come.

I pull out my notebook and I write to her like I write every day,

"Hey Best Friend . . .

I've lost eight pounds, but it's only been two weeks, don't get mad, I will gain them all back. I promise I will before I see you again. I'm trying to eat, I just feel so sick all of the time. It's hard to eat without crying, and it's hard to swallow food when you're crying . . . it's like sneezing with your eyes open. I guess it doesn't matter that much though, since our bodies are what we leave behind.

If that's true then how will you recognize me in Heaven?"

And as soon as the words hit the paper I already know that she will know exactly who I am by my soul not by my body and she will be throwing elbows past all of the other angels to be the first to greet me. She wouldn't knock anyone over, because that's just not heavenly behavior. But I know she would be there first.

No matter what.

Thinking about seeing her again makes me want to smile.

Thinking about how one day none of this will matter.

One day, we will all be gone.

And together we'll be the orchestrators of the winds that blow pinwheels and we'll be the welcoming committee for everyone else we love who comes after us.

And I look back at the grass around me and notice how even the short spikey blades are all pointing, reaching, for Heaven. How even the Earth itself is temporary.

None of this is permanent.

Even the clouds in the sky have changed paths from a few moments ago, they have bypassed each other and have made completely new shapes now. They already have a new story to tell. Above all, they tell me that the world is indeed still spinning. Still.

The world goes on around me, around death, and never stops.

Looking up at the clouds, my eyes are full. Life feels like both a daunting task and a privilege.

I close my notebook and finally let myself feel tired. I watch the pinwheels try to start, but they stop. I wish that they would just start and spin forever in never-ending motion.

When they stop it feels like her ending all over again.
But when they spin, I feel like she's going on somewhere . . .
And that I can go on too.

I put the big blue stuffed animal on the ground next to where her head might be, as if we were sharing a bed at one of our childhood sleepovers, and I lie down on top of the blue fuzzy lump. I curl up on my side and when I'm alone and vulnerable to the world outside, in the middle of the day, in the middle of the cemetery, I let myself do something I haven't done in days. I feel safe enough to sleep. At least here, when I wake up, I won't have to feel that she's gone.
I won't have to remember it.
I'll already be right here, next to her.

. . .

With the jolting sound of a car door closing I feel all the weight of time. My eyes blink open to see who might be visiting someone close by.
I'm surprised to see that the three shapes standing beside the car look familiar.
They are surprised too.
They stretch their necks to look around tombstones as if we are standing in a crowded room full of people and I sit up, and block the sun from my eyes with my hand.
"Hello?" Unsure, one of my aunts calls to me.
I can see her walk into view, and I nod my head, "Hi, it's just me . . ."
Guilty of being here.
Still.

I pick my notebook up and tidy up around me as if they were unexpected company walking through my front door. "I . . . I just came . . . to nap . . ." I realize that it sounds sad and pathetic. But I know that for now, for a while yet maybe, it will have to be okay that I'm just sad and pathetic. And maybe in time I will be able to add other adjectives to who I am; the "sad and pathetic" that I feel now will still be there . . . but they won't be the only things.

In time I will become other things.

I know I will.

"We just came to bring flowers . . ." My aunt bends over, looking at the rectangle patch of dirt lovingly before turning to me and asking, "How are you doing . . . ?"

My first reaction is to say *"I'm fine."* But I know that I'm not. I'm the furthest thing from fine.

I don't know that I'll ever be fine again, but I do know one thing, and that's if I say *"I'm fine"* enough, people will do the single most terrifying thing they could do; they will start to believe me.

So instead I just shake my head and shrug at the fresh flowers she's brought and try not to think about how even the most beautiful of flowers make me sad now.

"We are headed out to dinner, do you want to come?" My aunt tells me about the restaurant they're going to while setting the flowers down at the head of her niece's grave. She's trying to convince me with menu items, but all I can think about is the feeling of being trapped in a restaurant booth with too many feelings inside and none of them being hunger.

"No, that's okay. I'm not hungry." I shake my head.

She tells me that they are taking my little cousin to a movie afterwards and that I should come, and even if I don't eat I can see a movie with them.

I'm still shaking my head from the first invitation.

"You should come," she says again. And she says it in a way that makes me realize it's not about the chicken fingers or the burger selection or about how great or not great Angelina Jolie might be in the movie they're going to see. It's about not spending the rest of my night and the rest of my life setting up shop in the cemetery.

Life is about something more.

I know that.

It's just so hard.

261

And even though my heart, my body, and my mind are all still screaming "*No*," I nod my head "*Yes*."

Even though right now, spending the rest of my life in the cemetery is exactly what I feel like I should be doing.

And maybe, I think, maybe it will get easier.

Maybe I'll feel a little bit less dead every day.

Maybe someday I will say "yes" to things again and I will mean it. Maybe getting back to normal starts with chicken fingers and french fries. Maybe going on living just takes practice.

I draw in a deep breath.

Death has changed me, but I can't let it chain me down.

And even though I am still in my heart and soul fighting her death right now, I collect my things, I walk over to my car, and I get in.

I look down at my hand and open my palm to see that I'm still cupping the circular piece of metal, and I trace the outline of her car's emblem with my thumb. There are some things that are harder to let go of than others. Some things I'll never let go of completely. I know that. But still, I have anxiety about pulling away from the cemetery right now. It's still hard to leave her, even though it's not the first time or the last time I'll have to leave her again.

{Even though she's the one who really left first.}

Before I put the car into drive,
I look back at Makenzie's grave.

And all of the pinwheels,
Every single one of them,
Are spinning like they'll never stop.

Death will linger inside of you longer than it should, and it will come back around again in more ways than one, to take away parts of you that you thought you had already lost forever. Each new death that comes your way will bring back pain from every previous loss. You will once again mourn the person that you used to be, the person that you once were, before death changed you.

But you can't let the death around you bleed you of your life.
  You have to live through it.
    You have to move through it.
You just have to keep moving through to the end, and then on some more, just past the end. Because . . .

  Ends meet beginnings.
  Always.
  No matter what.

Epilogue

Tires roll over the tiny stones of the cemetery entrance without much traction. The tires on Faith's silver SUV are worn down by time and distance, they tell of all of the places she's been in the last ten years.

Faith pulls around to a familiar grassy section of the cemetery and notices how much things have changed since she's been here last. All of the bushes have been pulled from beside their family plot and she looks around to see that there is no longer any landscaping in the cemetery. It's only sky, earth, and tombstones now. The cemetery workers must not have been able to keep up with the landscaping. Maybe there's fewer people living that want to take care of the maintenance of the dead. Maybe they couldn't afford it in such a small cemetery. Faith shrugs off the reminder that nothing ever stays the same, and she takes a deep breath. She draws a sigh in as far as she can and pushes it out hard.

She parks in front of a familiar row of gravestones.

Before she gets out of her car, she grabs six loose roses and a bouquet. She closes her car door behind her and her painted toes gently lead her over to the grave in flip-flops.

Her feet slow beneath her as she gets closer.
Her heart gets heavy and her eyes get tight.
{Even after all this time.}

She takes a deep breath to try to slow her heart.
She takes another deep breath to try to hold back tears.
Reminding herself that this place isn't where Makenzie is anymore. That it was never really where she was at all. It's just the saddest of all of the places anyone can remember her now.

Faith kneels down inspecting all the things that are around Makenzie's marker and sighs at the silk flower wreath on display. From far away the silk arrangement looked bright and cheery, but up close Faith can see the fabric of the yellow flowers is frayed and the centers of the flowers are lacking. The living seem to have a lot of varying opinions about fake flowers.

Maybe they are better because they will never wilt and die.
But Faith thinks they are less for having never lived.

At least Makenzie lived.

And Faith draws another deep breath, knowing it's all the same. She's sure that Heaven doesn't care about the difference between fake flowers and real flowers. In Heaven they probably have some kind of much better version of flowers anyways, ones that sing music when they bloom maybe, and maybe to Heaven even our best real flowers seem fake and lacking.

She leans over Mackenzie's flat gravestone. Etched in beside Makenzie's name is a shooting star, and Faith rubs it, brushing off stale dirt that the wind and weather have attached to it, as she leans her face close to kiss the indent where the star is. As Faith leans over, the back of her tank top hikes up just slightly to show a tattoo on Faith's lower back with a matching shooting star. Under the star in black ink are the words, "No Regrets," in Mackenzie's handwriting.

Faith leans back from kissing Mackenzie's star, and her tank top re-covers the tattoo that has been etched into her body and into her soul.

Faith fans out six roses, a red, a white, a bright pink, a soft pink, an orange with red tips, and a peach, and lays them over the clover-populated grass in front of Makenzie's marker. Faith looks at the roses longingly, thinking about what kind of music the roses that grow in Heaven might sing.

She sits down, next to a familiar spot where she shared so many sunrises and sunsets. The cemetery itself feels like an old friend, something that was there for her when she needed an ear to listen and a place to go. Sitting down inside the cemetery now is comfortable in a way that she couldn't have imagined, the kind of comfort that only time and movement can bring to anything.

Faith pauses and looks at the gravestones around her. There's something about the way some of them from the 1800s have aged, so white in color, so faded, that makes Faith think about all the passing of time that has come and gone before her. And there's something about the newer stones made of granite and marble like Makenzie's that make her think about all of the time that will keep going long after she is gone.

And all of the stones put together make her think about the time that's going on right now.

Passing moment by moment.

She leans in, reaching over just a tad to set the extra bouquet of yellow sunflowers on the grass-covered plot next to Makenzie's. Time has taken more people away from Faith, but Earth's spinning gears have also brought more people into her life.

The plastic around the bouquet crinkles for only a second after it's laid down. Faith's eyes are set on the bouquet until she has the kind of anxiety that can only be calmed by putting pen to paper. Faith digs into her embroidered canvas tote bag and pulls out a peach notebook with a wishie on the cover. She drags the bottom of her tote like a lake looking for a pen. She finds one, and she opens to the next clean page in her journal. The pen pauses at the stale feeling of wanting nothing more than to tell Makenzie these things in person.

And Faith reminds herself that she will one day, but until then she's got to get it out of her and on to paper, not so much as before so that she won't forget, but more so to just let it out. Once they are out on paper, they can no longer have a hold over her.

Her hands rest between blank pages, setting the pen down to fall between the crease of the journal. The fingers on her right hand play with the engagement and wedding rings on the ring finger of her left hand, twisting them back and forth while she thinks about nothing and everything all at once. Faith thinks about her life and all the things that have changed in the last ten years. . . . There's something about the amount of time that has gone by that makes her feel like a survivor. There's something in the way that following her heart, despite it being perpetually broken, has made her feel like a success. Something about letting go of pain and letting love in has made her feel happy again. And there's something about choosing happiness that has made her the healthiest she has ever been.

Three large cut diamonds on her left hand reflect the sun and create tiny prisms of light, sending rainbows to dance across the blank journal page. And just as Faith notices the tiny rainbows, her attention is taken by two small white butterflies floating by.

It's taken some time, but it's finally rainbows and butterflies. Just like Makenzie always said it would be.

And Faith picks up the pen, and she writes:

"Hey Best Friend . . ."

Dear Reader,

Thank you for holding my story in your hands, allowing me to be vulnerable, and for coming on such an emotional journey with me. My heart was broken at eighteen when I first started writing this, and through these words (and tears) I've been able to find healing. There were parts of this book that were extremely hard to write (like . . . everything past the dedication page!). But, the one thing that kept me punching fingers to keys was the thought of you (yes, you!). The thought of you one day holding this in your hands and relating to even just one page, one paragraph, or one sentence that rang true to your life, your love, or your grief kept me moving and motivated to continue on, so—thank you.

I hope what you take away from this story inspires you. I hope that you continue on with your new beginning or maybe find inspiration to start one. I hope that if you do one thing tomorrow that you start journaling. You've got a story in you too. Don't let it only live inside of you. Don't let it eat you up. Even if you only write to do what Grandma says: "Write it down. Rip it up. And throw it away." You've got to let it out. Write about your day. Write about how you feel. Write about how you forgive someone. Write to someone you miss, even if they'll never read it. Write about your dreams for the future, and keep them close. Write anything, it doesn't have to be good, but just write, because, trust me on this, it's good for your soul.

And while you're writing, I'd love for you to write to me too. You can contact me at **heavenhasnoregrets@gmail.com** or at **www.HeavenHasNoRegrets.com**. You can also find some extras online such as deleted scenes, a soundtrack for the book, Book Club questions, and exclusive items inspired by Heaven Has No Regrets. Until we meet again—

*No Regrets,

Tessa

<u>*Links*</u>

Eating Disorders affect 30 million people across the United States. If you or someone you love is suffering with an eating disorder, find strength in knowing that you are not alone. For help with recovery, stories of hope, and support forums visit: **www.nationaleatingdisorders.org**

Promise me you'll always remember: You're braver than you believe, and stronger than you seem, and smarter than you think. ~ A.A. Milne

Grief is a journey. For "Creative Grieving" or to learn how to better support someone who's lost a loved one visit: **www.recover-from-grief.com**

To purchase personalized memorial jewelry and accessories created by the Author, visit: **www.MoonstoneCreation.Etsy.com**
"For All of Life's New Beginnings"

Acknowledgments

How often in life we complete a task that was beyond the capability of the person we were when we started it.
–Robert Brault

I have so much gratitude for the people in my life who have even at the smallest moment in time, been a source of inspiration, courage, or motivation. This book is an accumulation of my life and each person I've met along the way has somehow been an influence and a part of my journey leading me to where I am now—so if our paths have crossed, I thank you.

And although this book was primarily written alone, at a corner desk at 2 am, while the rest of the world was sleeping, it would not have come to be in print as it is now without the help of the following people:

To my husband, Shane Shaffer: Thank you for your un-ending patience, your unconditional love, and for always being my biggest fan. I would not be as sane, as grounded, or as ambitious if it weren't for your support. You've encouraged a story from my past to unfold in a way that I will always treasure, but my favorite story will forever and always be the one that we continue to write together.

To my mom and stepdad, Nadine and Gary Witmer: Thank you for believing in me and helping me to create my new beginning; none of my dreams would be coming true if it weren't for your love and support.

To my Grandma, Vera Radanovic: Thank you for being the best Grandma to everyone who knows you, and now to every reader who picks up this book as well. I will forever remember our talks, our laughs, and most of all—your hugs.

Thank you, Wendy Bolton, for not just your fantastic editing but for encouraging this story to come to life when it was only a few thoughts on a page eleven years ago. Thank you for helping me to dream again. Thank you for all of the adventures. I love you more than eating fried Mars bars in New York with the Pope on a day where it's raining-like-a-funeral but nobody dies.

Thank you, Jemma Church, for the amazing cover design of the book and the journal. Thank you for reading this book, re-reading it, reading it again, and providing crucial feedback every time. Thank you for reminding me of an important part of this story that I almost left out and for laughing with me about the parts of this story that were excluded on purpose. Most of all, thank you for being a part of this story—*"Because it was, you know. It was the best."*

Thank you, Mea Magaro, for your extremely helpful feedback on the very first completed draft. These characters and this book would not be what they are now without you. Thank you for your excitement for *Heaven Has No Regrets*, and for spreading your excitement and love of reading through teaching the future readers, writers, and authors of the world.

Thank you, Carrie Wagner, for your honest feedback and for being the tell-it-like-it-is kind of person that I love. Every writer should be so lucky to have a friend like you. Thank you most of all for inspiring the Epilogue— it is my favorite part of this book (and real life).

Thank you to Daria Milletics and Sarah Milletics for helping me brainstorm and settle on the character names; it was the biggest change in this story and such an important thing to get right. I couldn't love Faith and Makenzie more.

Thank you, Michele Anderson, for being a source of hope and encouragement. Thank you for reviewing and helping me further develop some of the most serious parts of this book. But thank you most of all for being the first person to make me laugh again. I didn't know how important that first laugh would be, but since then I have never, ever, forgotten it.

Also, Zach Forsburg: Thank you for helping share the story that caused that very first laugh, for sharing the dreamer's disease, and for always bringing the champagne.

Thank you, Sandy Shamansky, for allowing "the house that isn't mine" to be mine for a little while. 764 Erford will forever hold a special place in my heart for so many reasons. It was never really about that house though, it was about you. You will never know how much good you did for the kids who came to that house, who came to you. You were always there when we needed you, without judgment, without question, no matter what time of day or night, so on behalf of everyone who ever walked through the unlocked door of that house, I thank you.

It is with great love and gratitude that I thank Rickie Freedman for teaching me that we are all truly connected. Thank you for sharing and teaching me Usui Reiki, which has been a huge part of my continued physical, emotional, and spiritual healing process. Without Reiki, I can honestly say that I would not have been able to finish this book because I tried for nine years without progress. And without ReikiSpace I would not have met some of the amazing people who helped fuel me up along the road of my authorhood.

Thank you, Denise VanBriggle, for being my writing coach, my cheerleader, and for being the first person to ever call me an "Author" (even when this novel only existed in crinkled pages inside a binder). Thank you for the coffee dates that challenged me with deadlines, thank you for all of the guidance and feedback, and thank you for helping me dream of the day when this would become published.

Thank you, Andrew Morton, for seeing the stars and bringing me back to Earth when I thought this novel was "done." Thank you for helping me to realize that there was deeper to dig, more to move through, and things yet to face. And that even though this is "done" now, that this is still just another exciting beginning.

Finally,

To the boy with the goatee, the boy with the mohawk, the boy with the motorcycle, the boy with the baseball hat, the girl with the tattoos, the girl with the dimples, the girl with the cross around her neck, and the girl with the soft voice: Thank you. Although time and distance have come between some of us now, I want you to know that you've always been a special part of my heart and my life wouldn't be the same without having known you. Thank you for being there through the sunshine and the rain. Your friendship and love meant everything to me back then, and it still does now.

To the many others who lived through this story: Thank you for being a part of our journey, if even just for a little while. I know that reading this story and re-living these chapters has brought you many tears, but I hope that it has also brought healing. I hope that you can understand and hold on to the message that above all the heaviness of pain, anger, or guilt that this book may stir up here on Earth—that Heaven has

no regrets.

41731867R00156

Made in the USA
Charleston, SC
06 May 2015